Park Statue Politics

World War II Comfort Women Memorials in the United States

THOMAS J. WARD AND WILLIAM D. LAY

E-INTERNATIONAL RELATIONS PUBLISHING

E-International Relations
www.E-IR.info
Bristol, England
2019

ISBN 978-1-910814-50-5

This book is published under a Creative Commons CC BY-NC 4.0 license. You are free to:

- **Share** — copy and redistribute the material in any medium or format
- **Adapt** — remix, transform, and build upon the material

Under the following terms:

- **Attribution** — You must give appropriate credit, provide a link to the license, and indicate if changes were made. You may do so in any reasonable manner, but not in any way that suggests the licensor endorses you or your use.
- **NonCommercial** — You may not use the material for commercial purposes.

Any of the above conditions can be waived if you get permission. Please contact info@e-ir.info for any such enquiries, including for licensing and translation requests.

Other than the terms noted above, there are no restrictions placed on the use and dissemination of this book for student learning materials/scholarly use.

Production: Michael Tang
Cover Image: Yeongsik Im

A catalogue record for this book is available from the British Library.

E-IR Open Access

Series Editor: Stephen McGlinchey
Books Editor: Cameran Clayton
Editorial Assistants: Xolisile Ntuli and Shelly Mahajan

E-IR Open Access is a series of scholarly books presented in a format that preferences brevity and accessibility while retaining academic conventions. Each book is available in print and digital versions, and is published under a Creative Commons license. As E-International Relations is committed to open access in the fullest sense, free electronic versions of all of our books, including this one, are available on the E-International Relations website.

Find out more at: http://www.e-ir.info/publications

About E-International Relations

E-International Relations (E-IR) is the world's leading open access website for students and scholars of international politics, reaching over three million readers per year. E-IR's daily publications feature expert articles, blogs, reviews and interviews – as well as student learning resources. The website is run by a non-profit organisation based in Bristol, England and staffed by an all-volunteer team of students and scholars.

http://www.e-ir.info

Abstract

Numerous academics have researched Japan's dehumanizing comfort women system that, for decades, forced innocents into sexual slavery. Since 2010 a campaign has been in place to proliferate comfort women memorials in the United States. These memorials now span from New York to California and from Texas to Michigan. They recount only the Korean version of this history, which this text finds incomplete. They do not mention that, immediately following World War II, American soldiers also frequented Japan's comfort women stations. They say nothing of how, to the present day, GIs continue to patronize Asian women and girls organized in brothels near their barracks. The Korean narrative also ignores the significant role that Koreans played in recruiting women and girls into the system. Intentionally or not, comfort women memorials in the United States promote a political agenda rather than transparency, accountability and reconciliation.

Thomas J. Ward is Distinguished Dean Emeritus of the University of Bridgeport's College of Public and International Affairs. An honors graduate of the Sorbonne and a Phi Beta Kappa graduate of Notre Dame, he did his doctoral studies in Political Economy and International Education at the Catholic Institute of Paris and De La Salle University in the Philippines. He teaches graduate courses in International Conflict and Negotiation and Political and Economic Integration. A former Fulbright scholar, he has lectured at the Chinese Academy of Social Sciences in Beijing, and has been a Visiting Research Fellow at Academia Sinica in Taipei. His research on the comfort women issue has been published in *East Asia* and *Asia Pacific Journal: Japan Focus*.

William D. Lay is Director of the School of Public and International Affairs, and Chair, at the University of Bridgeport. He teaches graduate and undergraduate courses in international public law, international humanitarian law, US constitutional and criminal law, and human security. Born in Tokyo, he has traveled extensively in Asia and the Asia Pacific region. He was a Kent Scholar throughout his years at Columbia Law School, and was Senior Editor of the Columbia Law Review. He clerked at the New York Court of Appeals for Judge Joseph Bellacosa, a recognized authority on New York criminal procedure, and practiced law for 12 years with the Fried Frank and Skadden Arps firms in New York City before joining the UB faculty. His articles on East Asia have appeared in *East Asia* and the *Harvard Asia Quarterly*.

Contents

	INTRODUCTION	1
1.	LOCAL POLITICS: THE PROS AND CONS OF PARK STATUES	9
2.	THE ORIGINS AND IMPLEMENTATION OF THE COMFORT WOMEN SYSTEM	13
3.	STEPS TOWARD REDRESS FOR THE COMFORT WOMEN	27
4.	KEY MILEPOSTS AND ACTORS IN EFFORTS TO SETTLE THE ONGOING COMFORT WOMEN IMPASSE	35
5.	KOREAN CIVIL SOCIETY ORGANIZATIONS: ACCOMPLISHMENTS AND EXPECTATIONS	48
6.	OPPOSITION TO COMFORT WOMEN MEMORIALS IN THE UNITED STATES	64
7.	THE UNUSUAL CASE OF TAIWAN	79
8.	STATUE POLITICS VS. EAST ASIAN SECURITY: THE GROWING ROLE OF CHINA AND CHINESE-AMERICAN CIVIL SOCIETY	93
9.	INCONSISTENCIES IN THE KOREAN NARRATIVE	102
10.	THE COMFORT WOMEN CONTROVERSY IN THE AMERICAN PUBLIC SQUARE	112
11.	THE IMPLICATIONS OF ESTABLISHING A COMFORT WOMEN MEMORIAL IN THE UNITED STATES OR EUROPE	120
	CLOSING THOUGHTS	124
	NOTE ON INDEXING	126

Dedication

In the mid-1930s, the government of Japan established a government-controlled network of brothels, referred to as "ianjo" or comfort stations, based on a massive Japanese private prostitution network in place since the emergence of Japan as a colonial power in the late nineteenth century. The ianjo system involved the deployment of tens of thousands of indentured Japanese sex workers across Northern Asia.

As Japan prepared for war in the late 1930s, its military decided against continuing to recruit Japanese women for this purpose. The government replaced them largely with innocent Korean women and girls who joined the military because, in most cases, they had been deceptively recruited based on promises of a bright future with education and respectable, gainful employment. Instead these women became the exploited sex prisoners of the Japanese Army and the collaborators who had misled them into an unending nightmare of terror and rape.

This book is dedicated to the tens of thousands of women and girls who endured such deception only to face daily, multiple sexual violations by the Japanese military during World War II. Let us also remember the empty, ruined lives that surviving victims faced when they returned home after the war. They became marginalized from society because they had committed the "crime" of being raped.

Sadly, the role played by Korean, Chinese, and Taiwanese collaborators in the deceptive recruitment of women and girls for Japan's comfort women system must also be told. Just as the Croat, Serb, and Romanian nationals who oversaw Hitler's concentration camps did not escape judgment because they too were "victims." The crimes of the comfort system collaborators should not be concealed when the comfort women's story is told.

We should not forget that the American military also had a role in all of this. They patronized the comfort women system during the first year after the war. After that, for 72 years until today, American GIs have patronized the hundreds of thousands of women and girls trapped in the camp towns around U.S. bases in Japan, Korea, and the Philippines. Like the WWII comfort women, many of these women's lives have also been destroyed.

Nor can we forget that today, North Korean women escape every day across the border into China. To repay the "debt" for their "freedom," these women will be sold into a forced marriage or to a brothel in China. Many will face the same personal shock and terror that women and girls endured three-quarters of a century ago under Japan's military during the Pacific War.

Human trafficking extends far beyond Asia. By properly telling the story of the comfort women and properly identifying all responsible parties, we believe that we can best contribute to a future world where all women will experience that personal dignity, respect, and genuine love that the comfort women could never know.

Acknowledgments

This book explains, critiques, and expands on the competing state and civil society narratives regarding the dozen memorials erected in the United States since 2010 to honor female victims of the comfort women system established and maintained by the Japanese military from 1937 to 1945. We are grateful to University of Bridgeport President Neil Albert Salonen and Provost Dr. Stephen Healey for their support of our efforts over the past three years, and for the numerous University of Bridgeport faculty and students who have reviewed the materials in written or presentation form and given their helpful comments. We would like to thank Mr. Jonathan Stupple for all of the assistance he provided in the copyediting of the text. We also thank Chen Yen-Ju, librarian of Academia Sinica, as well as Eunjin Hong, Lily Shapiro, and Rebecca Bruckenstein of the University of Bridgeport for their help in verifying sources and preparing preliminary drafts. A special thank you is given to Ms. Moriko Hori, a Columbia University graduate from Japan and president of the Japan Chapter of the Women's Federation for World Peace, who assisted us in our preliminary research on this topic, and to University of Bridgeport students Chang Sheng-ping and Dan Rabottini who helped with translation work.

We also wish to express our special appreciation for Taiwan's Ministry of Foreign Affairs and Karen Chu of the Taipei Economic and Cultural Office for arranging Dr. Ward's travel and stay in Taipei to research Taiwan-Japan relations and the unique case of Taiwanese WWII comfort women. It was fortuitous to share findings and work closely with Academia Sinica's Institute of Modern History Research Fellow Wen-Tang Shiu, a tremendous mentor and support, as well as Dr. Miaw-fen Lu, Director of Academia Sinica's Institute of Modern History, Dr. Ming-Chang Tsai, the Director of Academia Sinica's Center for Asia-Pacific Area Studies, and other Academia Sinica research scholars especially Dr. Chu Te-lan, the pioneer of Taiwanese comfort women studies, Dr. Parris Chang, Pennsylvania State University Professor Emeritus and former member of the Taiwan Legislative Yuan, Dr. Lung-chih Chang of National Taiwan University, Dr. Wen-Ji Wang of National Yang-Ming University, Ms. Lily Lin and Joyce Lin Juoyu of Tamkang University, as well as Ms. Kang Shu-hwa, Executive Director of the Taipei Women's Rescue Foundation.

Many thanks also to our families and friends.

Foreword

In March 2017, Europe's first comfort women memorial was dedicated in Wiesent, Germany, a small town in Bavaria with a population of approximately 2,500. The monument was described in the *Korea Times* as the "first 'comfort women' statue in Europe," suggesting that there could be more in the future. The *Korea Times* reported that, on the one hand, this statue along with the 60 some other statues that have already been set up in Korea, China, Canada, the United States and Australia served "as a means to promote global awareness of comfort women," that is, the tens of thousands of women and girls forced into sexual slavery by Japan's military during WWII. The *Korea Times* added that the comfort women statues also stand "in protest of the deal reached between Seoul and Tokyo on the issue in December 2015,"[1] the date when the agreement was signed by Japan and Korea which in theory ended the comfort women impasse between the two countries. This agreement fell apart with the March 2017 impeachment of Korean President Park Geun-hye. Park was the key Korean proponent of the deal whereby Japan recognized that the Japanese military leadership was directly responsible for the creation of the comfort women system and it agreed to provide some $8.3 million for the creation of a foundation to provide support for surviving comfort women.

The events surrounding the installation of the Wiesent statue provide insight into our motivation for writing this book. In fact, on September 8, 2016, the sister cities of Suwon, Korea and Freiburg, Germany announced plans for the installation of the first comfort woman statue in Europe. The statue's dedication was set for December 10, 2016, to coincide with the commemoration of International Human Rights Day.[2] Freiburg is a city 100 times larger than Wiesent. Wiesent was approached only after Freiburg rescinded its decision to install the statue just two weeks after having announced the plan to go forward. Freiburg leaders reversed themselves because of the stiff resistance they faced from their Japanese sister city of Matsuyama.[3]

Korean civil society groups almost certainly do not plan to limit their comfort

---

[1] Bo-eun Kim, "Europe's First Comfort Women Statue Set up in Germany," *The Korea Times,* March 9, 2017, http://www.koreatimes.co.kr/www/nation/2018/02/120_225355.html.

[2] "Europe's First 'Comfort Women' Statue Planned for German City, *The Japan Times*, September 8, 2016, https://www.japantimes.co.jp/news/2016/09/08/national/plan-afoot-install-europes-first-comfort-women-statue-freiburg/#.WsvAcy7waUl.

[3] "German City Drops Plan to Install First 'Comfort Women' Statue in Europe," *The Japan Times*, September 22, 2016, https://www.japantimes.co.jp/news/2016/09/22/national/german-city-drops-plan-install-first-comfort-women-statue-europe/#.WpHTN67iaUk.

women statue installations to just one country in Europe or to just one city in Germany. They hope to see a proliferation of comfort women statues there as a platform for their narrative of the comfort women's story. In the United States, in less than a decade, comfort women statues have spread from New Jersey to California and from Michigan to Texas. And, as with Freiburg and Wiesent, city officials have found themselves caught up in a war of memory between opposing camps.

Like Europe, America had nothing to do with the creation of the comfort women system. Most Americans know virtually nothing about this chapter of history. The decision by Freiburg to rescind its plan for a comfort women memorial suggests that, like their American counterparts, European political leaders may be caught off guard and not know enough to take an educated position on the comfort women. Other parts of the world invited to join this debate may also find that they have a limited understanding of this period in East Asian history.

In May 2017, Japan's financial maneuvers with the United Nations Educational, Scientific, and Cultural Organization (UNESCO) blocked inclusion of damning comfort women records in that organization's official "Memory of the World" historical archives. As it had done in 2016, the Japanese government postponed release of a monetary contribution of $30.84 million to the organization pending UNESCO's review of an application from Chinese, South Korean, and Japanese civic groups for adding a "Voices of the Comfort Women" archival collection in UNESCO's Memory of the World program. The "Voices" collection recounts what women endured as military sex slaves of the Japanese Empire. It inculpated Japan's WWII government and decried today's Japan for continuing to obstruct justice for the surviving victims.[4]

On October 16, 2017, instead of supporting the "Voices of the Comfort Women" proposal, the Memory of the World International Advisory Committee called in its communiqué for dialogue between those who had submitted this proposal and competing Japanese and American non-governmental organizations (NGOs) that had submitted their own exculpatory version of this history to UNESCO in a proposal entitled "Documentation on 'Comfort Women' and Japanese Army Discipline."[5] The UNESCO advisory committee expressed hope for an eventual "joint nomination to encompass as far as

---

[4] Ki-weon Cho, "Japan Again Withholds Annual Funding to UNESCO Memory of the World," *Hankyoreh*, May 8, 2017, http://english.hani.co.kr/arti/english_edition/e_international/793834.html.

[5] "International Memory of the World Register Recommended Nominations List 2016–2017," UNESCO, https://en.unesco.org/sites/default/files/mow_recommended_nominations_list_2016-2017.pdf.

possible all relevant documents."⁶

Not only the United States but also UNESCO, Taiwan, Canada, Australia, and Germany as well as other parts of Europe have found or may soon find themselves parties to the unsettled debate over the historical memory of the comfort women. Countries and organizations find themselves forced to choose between the delimited Korean narrative of historical events versus the equally delimited Japanese narrative. Through the "hide and seek" maneuvers of Korea and Japan, the two major players in this dispute, pyrrhic victories are scored with setbacks for both sides in other battles that ensue.

This book focuses on the history of the comfort women system as well as on the American experience with comfort women statues. With some fifteen memorials established since 2010, the United States has far more comfort women memorials than any other country in the world except for Korea. There are also numerous American cities that have balked until now at establishing comfort women memorials. These include Washington, D.C., Atlanta, New York City, and Detroit. One reason for hesitance is the strong, official Japanese opposition to such memorials. American municipal leaders must engage and decipher the truth of two conflicting comfort women narratives, one promoted by Korean advocates and the other by the Japanese government, each with active support from Korean-American and Japanese-American civil society actors. As a result of this caustic debate, players on the Korean, the Japanese, and the American sides of the dispute have all suffered adverse consequences.

Japan and the Republic of Korea are America's two most important Pacific allies in facing the challenges of a nuclearized North Korea as well as those posed by China, an emerging military superpower interested in consolidating its claims to Taiwan, to the South China Sea, and to the Diaoyu/Senkaku Islands. Because of the comfort women controversy, Japan and Korea were not on speaking terms for several years. Still today they compete in embittered public relations offensives. Viewers were reminded of these tensions at the 2018 Winter Olympics in Pyeongchang, Korea. At the beginning of the competition, the National Broadcasting Company network (NBC) issued a written apology to the Korean organizers and it also dismissed its political commentator Joshua Cooper Ramo for saying, "every Korean will tell you that Japan is a cultural, technological and economic example that has been so important to their own transformation." NBC took these steps after the Pyeongchang Olympic Organizing Committee objected and "informed NBC of the errors in their commentary and the sensitivity of the

---

⁶ "International Memory of the World Register Recommended Nominations List 2016–2017," UNESCO.

subject in Korea." [7]

The prime targets of Japan's and Korea's public relations efforts in the United States have largely been local American mayors and city councils, typically from small towns, admittedly not as small as Wiesent, Germany but not major metropolitan centers.[8] Leaders in such municipalities often deal with policies on taxes, zoning, loitering, solicitation, the sale of alcohol, parking rules, garbage disposal, recycling and the setting of fines for failing to pick up after one's dog. Yet local leaders have now been thrust into a complicated historical, sociocultural, and political debate on whether or not to install a statue in a city park that will denounce Japan and honor the memory of the Asian women who, some 80 years ago, were forced into sexual slavery by Japan and dispatched to military brothels in places such as India, China, Burma, Indonesia, and the Philippines. The municipal leaders of these American towns need to decide whether the allegations against Japan are accurate. They must then decide whether or not to dedicate a monument to the comfort women victims in a local park, a park that likely has no monument to many closer-to-home atrocities such as African slavery or the annihilation of Native Americans.

American leaders seem to have made judgment calls on the comfort women issue without a broader understanding of the many factors involved in this tragic chapter of East Asian history. The narratives used to lobby for and against comfort women statues in the United States provide no "teaching moment." They ignore the cultural attitudes, mindset, and conditions that allowed for this cruel exploitation to occur in the first place. Intentionally or not, the inscriptions used on the memorials indict only one country, when, one could argue that culpability extends beyond Japan. Furthermore, in light of today's massive ongoing trafficking of women and girls in Japan, China, and Korea, it is tragic that the monuments fail to inform Americans of this, especially because many of the Filipina and Russian women who staff the brothels used by American military personnel in Northeast Asia are the products of such trafficking. The monuments in America denounce the trafficking of a century past in detail using contested numbers and descriptions of how women were coerced into service. They at best offer lip service to the victims of today's trafficking and serve to fuel the short-sighted

---

[7] Liana Baker, "NBC Apologise and Remove Joshua Cooper Ramo from Air following Comments about South Korea and Japan," *The Independent,* February 12, 2018, http://www.independent.co.uk/sport/olympics/winter-olympics/joshua-cooper-ramo-removed-sacked-nbc-apologise-japan-korea-comments-winter-olympics-2018-a8206216.html.

[8] The first comfort women memorial in the United States was established in 2010 in Palisades Park, New Jersey, which at the time had a population of 19,622. The only major American city that has a comfort women memorial at time of writing is San Francisco, California.

political agendas and ambitions of male politicians (and some females as well) in Korea, Japan, China, the United States, Australia, and perhaps now in Germany.

There is much that the leaders of municipalities all over the world can and should learn from the comfort women statue experiences of the United States. This text breaks new ground in studying both the process and the implications of having local government leaders take positions on competing historical narratives of events that took place almost 70 years ago. In our research, we have relied on the groundbreaking research that brought the comfort women issue to the forefront in the 1990s. This begins with the pioneering work of Yoshimi Yoshiaki who provided a documented confirmation of the existence of the Japanese Imperial Army's comfort women system and its mode of operation. Yuki Tanaka provided further elaborations on the system but he also confirmed its historical precedents and its continuance following the war with the assent of the leadership of U.S. Military Occupation forces. In this book, we also recognize C. Sarah Soh for her contribution to the wider narrative that inculpates actors beyond Japan. We regret not having been able to meet with her during our visit last summer to California to visit key sites there.

Our research includes a compendium of texts on the ordeals faced by the comfort women. This includes all of the testimonies of the survivors who endured the comfort women system that have been compiled by the Korean Council for the Women Drafted for Military Sexual Slavery by Japan, by the Taipei Women's Rescue Foundation, and by Japan's Asia Women's Forum. It also includes the testimony of Filipina comfort woman Rosa Henson, the testimonies of mainland Chinese women prepared by Dr. Peipei Qiu, and the official testimony and remembrances of Jan Ruff-O'Herne, a Dutch woman who was forced into the system.

In an attempt to get a better understanding of the United States' handling of the system, we also examined the archives and official correspondences available between the United States and Japan in the years leading up to the war that are located in Franklin Delano Roosevelt Presidential Library in Hyde Park, New York. This included communications by representatives of the Korean independence movement with the White House. We have also pored over the legal proceedings of cases brought against Japan by comfort women both in American and in Japanese courts, as well as to the responses to such allegations, and to the campaign to proliferate comfort women statues by the Global Alliance for Historical Truth led by Dr. Koichi Mera.

As long as the comfort women issue remains in contention, arguments over the veracity of the Japanese versus the Korean account of this chapter of Pacific War history will be played out over and over again in small towns and villages across the United States. We have necessarily been reliant on local news coverage and television coverage of those matters. Such developments are a fundamental concern of this text. They have led us to make first-hand visits to comfort women memorials in New Jersey (including the very first comfort women memorial in the world which was dedicated in 2010 in Palisades Park), New York, Virginia, and California, including the Glendale statue and the site of the newly installed San Francisco statue.

Over the past four years, we have also had the opportunity to report on and present our findings to experts in the field at conferences in Connecticut, Washington, DC, and in Taipei, Taiwan. Our research has produced articles for the *East Asia Quarterly* and the *Asia-Pacific Journal: Japan Focus*. All research and experiences have helped us to collect our thoughts, refine them and produce here what we believe will be a valuable text for scholars, NGO leaders, and local political leaders in the U.S. and in other parts of the world who are asked to take sides on a chapter of history of which they know very little. The decisions they make can lead to unanticipated social and geopolitical ramifications, and we hope to shed light on all considerations.

Introduction

The Competing Narratives of Statue Politics

In October 2010, James Rotundo, the mayor of Palisades Park, New Jersey, a city with a population of approximately 20,000 people, made a decision that greatly pleased his constituents of whom more than half are of Korean heritage. Rotundo agreed that it made sense to set up a monument just outside the Palisades Park Public Library to honor the victims of Japan's WWII comfort women system, that is, a Japanese government-supported system that inducted women and girls into a coercive network to provide sexual services to members of the Japanese military. The majority of these women were of Korean origin. The monument in Palisades Park depicts a Korean woman dressed in a traditional Korean dress known as a *Hanbok*. The woman is being whipped by a Japanese soldier.

James Rotundo is not an expert on Korean-American or Korean-Japanese relations. Actually he has only a high school degree. Nevertheless, he was convinced that his decision, some 65 years after the war, to set up what Japanese government officials viewed as an anti-Japanese monument was the right thing to do. The phenomenon of municipal and county officials creating memorials to the victims of the WWII comfort women system, based on a carefully scripted narrative of events of which they have little direct knowledge or experience has repeated itself in towns and counties across the United States from New York to California and from Texas to Michigan. Decisions have repeatedly been made by Americans politicians with no expertise in the events surrounding this tragic chapter of history. Ironically, minor American political leaders are setting up anti-Japanese monuments in the United States, apparently having forgotten that, unlike Korea, the United States is itself directly responsible for the round-up and detention of more than 100,000 Japanese-Americans in the early 1940s. One also wonders why these American officials felt justified in condemning Japanese atrocities in the comfort women monuments while failing to mention that, even seven decades after the end of WWII, U.S. military forces in East Asia continue to use Japanese, Korean, and Filipina women and girls as their "comfort women."

This book does not deny the reality of Japan's comfort women system nor does it question Japan's central role or the system's impropriety and cruelty; however, it does invite reflection on whether or not the mayors of mostly small American towns and villages should, based on limited information, decry the guilt of Japan alone when, this book asserts, there is "plenty of guilt to spread around." Indeed, we argue here that while Japan was unquestionably the principal perpetrator, Korea and America are not without blame, especially when seen in the broader context of the misogynous mentality and behaviors that characterized this chapter of history. We hope to establish through this text that municipal, state, and federal officials in the United States, as well as non-profit organizations that work to address justice and human rights, find themselves drawn into a debate on a subject about which they often know very little beyond the narratives put forth by pro-Korean and pro-Japanese advocacy groups, which seek support in establishing monuments to honor WWII "comfort women" or prevent their proliferation.

The Korean narrative supporting the comfort women statues, politicians, educators and civil society organizations (CSOs) tells that hundreds of thousands of women and girls, some as young as 14, were taken away from their homes in Korea and Taiwan and shipped off as far away as Indonesia, Burma, or the Mariana Islands to provide sexual services to the Japanese military, for sometimes dozens of soldiers each day. Many of these women perished during the closing months of the war on remote battlefields including Saipan, Iwo Jima, and Okinawa. Survivors of the comfort women system struggled with permanent physical or psychological damage after WWII because of the abuse and mistreatment that they endured for years as comfort women. Many lost the ability to bear children. And in Korea, a nation that made female virginity a requisite for marriage eligibility, survivors felt too ashamed to even think about finding a spouse or having a family once they returned home. They instead resorted to prostitution after the war or became hidden-away second spouses. Others lived on their own, selling Korean kimchi or other goods, trying to escape the nightmares of the hidden months or years of shame of the comfort women system that had broken their spirits.

Comfort women advocates have occasionally been accompanied by one of the very few survivors of the ordeal. These women are now in their eighties and nineties. They understandably harbor feelings of resentment and outrage towards Japan which, they feel, has offered only watered-down admissions of culpability and, on more than one occasion, has threatened even to retract those. Japan is criticized by Korea for not making an official apology and for failing to offer official compensation to the victims.

Korean advocacy groups, focusing on towns and counties where Korean-

Americans have political leverage, work with local politicians to gain support for the building of a memorial to the comfort women in the venue in question. Municipalities are usually not asked to fund the monument; private Korean-American citizens or even local municipal governments in Korea commit to cover costs for its creation and design. The rationale for a monument's presence in an American town or city is that it represents an important statement of support not only for the survivors of the system who remain, but also for today's victims of human trafficking and sexual slavery. Comfort women advocates and their government supporters also do understand that the erection of these monuments serve to pressure and embarrass Japan for not fully grappling with its past and recognizing its culpability for these crimes.

After setting up his city's memorial, Palisades Park's Mayor James Rotundo had his ticket to Korea, where he met with survivors in the comfort women's House of Sharing, a special residency for survivors, paid for by one group. Other politicians have also been the beneficiaries of paid trips to Korea. For many others, the extent of direct contact may simply be a local meeting, which occasionally can begin with a complementary home-made Korean dinner.

More than a dozen towns and counties in the United States have established comfort women memorials. Other locales continue to be lobbied to make this same symbolic gesture of support for the comfort women. These memorials, nevertheless, clearly take a full-throttled swipe at Japan. The 2010 plaque honoring the comfort women in Palisades Park, New Jersey has an inscription that reads as follows:

> In memory of the more than 200,000 women and girls who were abducted by the armed forces of the government of Imperial Japan 1930s–1945 known as 'Comfort Women.' They endured human rights violations that no peoples should leave unrecognized. Let us never forget the horrors of crimes against humanity.

Mayors, members of city councils, and even members of the U.S. Congress find themselves in the position to support or oppose such proposals. The temptation is always there to make that determination based on weighing the political pros and cons. If the Korean-American CSO that approaches a politician represents a key voting bloc of his or her city or county, the politician will understand the potential pay-off in satisfying the group's request. Koreans are hard-working people and one of America's most successful immigrant populations.[1] They have made their mark by rising to the top in law, medicine,

---

[1] "The Korean American Success Story," *BBC News*, March 30, 2011, http://www.bbc.

business, and other professional fields. Civil society organizations dealing with issues such as human trafficking could intuit that if they support the comfort women advocates, they, in turn, may receive reciprocal support for a project that they value in the future. Beyond benefits that may be inured, human rights organizations would understandably be concerned about the violations of human dignity and rights that resulted from the dehumanizing policy of the comfort women system and would be naturally inclined to denounce it for stealing away the lives of tens of thousands of women and girls.

As these efforts become more publicly known, Japanese-American CSOs may also approach these same political and civil society leaders. In some cases, even Japanese diplomats may become involved, as they were in Palisades Park, New Jersey, Glendale, California, and Fairfax County, Virginia. These talented diplomats present a radically different narrative and contend that comfort women interest groups misrepresent the actual unfolding of events. These diplomats provide what seems to be credible evidence to the contrary, arguing, for example, that the women and girls were not, in fact, abducted by the Japanese military. They provide testimonies from some comfort women who testified that they were "well-paid" and who maintain that they became involved in the system voluntarily. They describe how the women lived in comfortable quarters and were made fully aware of what awaited them when they agreed to join the Japanese war effort as sex workers in the first place.

They may also argue that it is unfair to criticize Japan alone. They may argue that the Korean procurers of these women, and the American military officials who, after WWII, chose not to prosecute those responsible for the mistreatment of the comfort women, share the blame with Japan. They will no doubt mention that Korea created its own comfort women system after WWII. They may also elaborate on the legal complaints filed against the Korean government by women who claim they were coerced by Korean officials to serve as prostitutes in the camp towns surrounding U.S. military bases in Korea since the time of the presidency of Park Chung-hee. They may even refer to the thousands of Vietnamese women who have filed complaints regarding the sexual abuse they suffered at the hands of Korean soldiers during the Vietnam War.

What are responsible local leaders to believe? They are not experts in East Asian history. They have probably never studied the Japanese or Korean language. Yet they suddenly find themselves pressured from both sides to be judges of a chapter of history of which they often know very little. This book

com/news/world-us-canada-12888908.

suggests that academics, politicians, and civil society leaders alike must assess their qualifications to decide on this matter. They need to weigh the impact that their statement of support or the decision not to support the erection of a memorial may have both locally and internationally.

The tragic chronicle of the comfort women is multi-layered and complex. Thus far, a number of U.S. municipalities have failed to recognize the need for a nuanced approach in addressing this matter. The memorial in Palisades Park, New Jersey, for example, states that the norm for the comfort women was to be *abducted from their homes*. The hundreds of testimonies of survivors, however, show that most victims were lured into the system through deceptive promises of career training and education; they were not "abducted."

In Glendale, California, a plaque next to the comfort women statue has a heading in a larger font than the rest of the inscription: "I was a sex slave of Japanese military." Intentionally or not, this statement deprecates one of Glendale's ethnic minorities. Further, the Glendale City Council was not fully informed of the text of the plaque at the time of the statue's approval, circumstances that led to litigation against the city. Council members were presented only a schematic diagram depicting the monument. When City Council member Ara Najarian asked what language would appear on the plaque, staff member Dan Bell merely stated that it would be "some general language commemorating comfort women."[2] The court acknowledged that the City Council approved the monument without knowing the inscription's content, but ruled that the decision to defend the lawsuit was a *de facto* approval of the inscription, even with the heading, "I was a sex slave of Japanese military."[3] The resolution's sponsors seemed to have forgotten that some survivors of the WWII internment camps that detained Japanese-Americans called Glendale home.[4]

America has recently experienced a deep divide over Confederate memorials. One lesson learned from the debate surrounding them is that monuments that serve to perpetuate carefully crafted, yet inaccurate or incomplete historical narratives may not survive into the future. Local politicians need to "get it right." Elected officials, particularly local officials, determine tax rates, secure public safety, oversee municipal parks and public facilities. Local officials

---

[2] *Gingery v. City of Glendale*, 2016 Cal. App. Unpub. LEXIS 8375 (Cal. Ct. App. Nov. 23, 2016).
[3] *Gingery v. City of Glendale*, 2016 Cal. App. Unpub. LEXIS 8375 (Cal. Ct. App. Nov. 23, 2016).
[4] *See, e.g.,* Katherine Yamada, ««Verdugo Views: Glendale Recalls the Hardship of Japanese Internment Camps»,» Glendale News Press, Dec. 2, 2015.

often must turn their attention to menial tasks such as assuring that alternate day parking rules during snow season make sense. If they act either to build or to refrain from building a memorial to Korea's comfort women based on an inaccurate narrative, in spite of the best intentions of the parties who share them, this could backfire, especially at a time when the violations of women's rights increasingly become a pivotal topic in the United States.

What other information beyond that introduced by Japanese and Korean interest groups should be weighed in making a decision on whether or not to support the establishment of a memorial to the comfort women in a given jurisdiction? Should it matter to local government officials in the United States that the ongoing proliferation of anti-Japanese memorials in the United States may adversely affect U.S.-Japan relations? Have the leaders of a given municipality considered whether or not they or the municipality might face litigation for causing Japanese-Americans to feel uncomfortable or unsafe due to a monument?

And what of the U.S. military's involvement with the comfort women following WWII? Have Korean-American CSOs reminded the small town decision-makers where monuments have been established that U.S. soldiers took advantage of the comfort stations in Japan during the first year of the occupation after the war? Is there sufficient awareness that for decades, on a large-scale, U.S. soldiers took advantage of Korean and Japanese girls and women pressured into prostitution because of their impoverished circumstances after WWII? Should any memorial intended to uphold justice and prevent future violence against women focus only on one perpetrator? Have local government officials weighed whether or not installation of comfort women monuments will lead to retaliatory memorials? Will these monuments next lead to statues honoring the women and girls in Korea, Japan, Vietnam, and the Philippines who have been abused by American military stationed in those countries for the past 70 years? We may have begun our way down a very long "slippery slope." Perhaps that is the right course, but careful consideration of all the facts is more than warranted.

This book invites readers to develop a deeper understanding of the competing narratives behind efforts to proliferate or oppose comfort women memorials around the United States. The authors identify two competing narratives on the comfort women experience. One is the Korean narrative, which, replete with testimonies from victims, indicts Japan's leadership from eight decades ago for the implementation of a system of sexual slavery. It calls for a direct, official apology from the highest level of Japan's current government and for official compensation for the tiny handful of surviving comfort women. The Japanese counter-narrative downplays Japan's level of guilt, suggests that most women joined the system voluntarily, and invites skepticism regarding the number of women involved and the living conditions that they faced. It also argues that Japan has already made sufficient attempts to both compensate the comfort women and to convey a sincere apology. Some Japanese further argue that there is more than enough guilt to spread around and that responsibility for the system should not be limited to Japan.

In this text, while introducing the history of comfort women and discussing their plight, we outline the weaknesses in the arguments that are presented on both sides. We assess how those weaknesses affect the narrative and the outcome of the conflict. We point to the role of the United States in this conflict and to the ways in which America's role needs to be included in the narrative. We also call for further reflection on the impact that these memorials can have on regional security, especially in East Asia where a non-democratic China continues to strengthen its military and economic influence.

Our efforts and the story we share here, we feel, expand the narrative of the comfort women. What results is a third narrative, distinct from the Korean and the Japanese rendering of events, and is what we refer to as an American narrative.

A decision to support the erection of a comfort women memorial in any American community based solely on the Korean account of events or a decision not to do so based solely on the Japanese apologia will not only impact local communities, but may also impact global affairs. Based on its catapulting economy and massive military build-up, China expects to soon rival the United States in global influence. China's November 2014 unilateral declaration of a greatly expanded Air Defense Identification Zone infringed on the territorial sovereignties of the governments of Korea, Japan, and Taiwan; in so doing, China showed blatant disregard for its neighbors. China has forcefully taken control of disputed islands in the South China Sea, and created artificial islands for airstrips and forward military placements. China also continues show trials of activists, threatens Hong Kong for seeking autonomy or independence, and provides indirect support for the military build-up of North Korea. Actions taken by American municipalities and NGOs can undermine coordinated Korean-Japanese-American initiatives to encourage China's "peaceful rise" based on rule of law rather than "the barrel of a gun" formula set in place by Mao.[5]

---

[5] Mao Tse Tung, "Quotations from Mao Tse Tung," trans. David Quentin and Brian Baggins, Marxists Internet Archive, https://www.marxists.org/reference/archive/mao/works/red-book/ch05.htm.

To conclude, we are not denialists. Evidence is manifest that many tens of thousands of Korean women were deceptively recruited or forced into sexual servitude in the years leading up to and throughout WWII. They were victims of egregious, fundamental violations of human rights during the war. We are not calling for an end to comfort women statues in the United States. We are proposing that, when they are built, they do what they purport to do: speak the truth, honor the wronged, and help to prevent future violations. Perhaps monuments in the United States that honor the comfort women should also expose the wrongdoing of the non-Japanese actors who helped to facilitate recruitment or allowed the system to survive the war and morph into the camp towns that serve U.S. military even today. Based on three years of research, we present a compelling case to invite decision-makers entrapped in "park statue politics" to pause and examine the impact of the past six years' worth of comfort women memorials. The information we have compiled invites a new and broader reflection on the events surrounding the comfort women. Japan and Korea continue to number among the developed countries that are most susceptible to brutal spousal abuse. For their part, American soldiers continue to patronize the brothels once populated by Korean and Japanese women and now often staffed by Filipinas and Russians within walking distance of U.S. military bases in Korea and Japan. China conveniently ignores the "comfort women" system within its borders that is staffed by North Korean female refugees. Faced with the debt incurred to escape to China, these women must choose between being sold off as brides to unmarried Chinese males or serving as indentured sex workers in brothels where they endure daily rape and humiliation.

In this book, we examine the arguments being brought forth to American municipal, state, and federal decision-makers regarding comfort women issues. We also consider whether or not the extant Korean and Japanese narratives on this matter suffice to formulate a satisfactory American response.

1

Local Politics: The Pros and Cons of Park Statues

The United States remains the most important ally of Japan and of Korea. The Japanese and Korean economies have so rapidly developed not only because of the remarkable entrepreneurial spirit of these two gifted populations, but also because the United States opened its markets and accepted the restrictions placed upon America's own manufacturers as they entered Japanese and Korean markets. Over time, the economies of Japan and Korea have emerged as the economic powerhouses they are today.

These two crucial American allies in Asia are now engaged in a war of memory, and America is a new battleground in that war. Those lobbied by Korean or Japanese interest groups have been identified as decision-makers or parties with leverage. Politicians who are contacted by comfort women advocacy groups have been chosen because they can introduce or offer support for legislation for the creation of a memorial in the town, city or state where they serve. Because two conflicting narratives exist on the objectivity and propriety of these memorials, political leaders have found themselves approached and pressured by both sides. They must choose whether to honor the victims as wished by the Korean advocates or prevent the approval of a memorial that, they have been convinced, will unfairly demean Japan. This scenario has repeated itself dozens of times in the United States since 2010. The decision taken by a municipality, regardless of how small it may be will have an impact on relations between Korea and Japan, and, when the resolution to establish a memorial is accepted, it also understandably stirs a bitter reaction towards the United States in certain parts of Japan, including very possibly the leadership of Japan's ruling party.

The Pursuit of Justice for Unpunished Crimes

We will examine this in greater detail in the later sections of the book, but let us begin by seeing this from the perspective of "leverage" and the role that leverage plays in the ongoing debate over Japan's treatment of the comfort women. In negotiations, we examine the leverage that each side possesses in the process. Leverage leads the opposing side in a conflict to recognize the importance of reaching a settlement. When the treatment of women and girls by the Japanese military came to the surface in the 1990s, it led to a groundswell of righteous rancor towards Japan, especially on the part of Koreans. A large portion of the women conscripted to serve as *ianfu,* or comfort women, during WWII came from Korea.

The first recourse that the victims sought beginning in the early 1990s was through the court system. Yet, during the 14 year period between 1991 and 2005, few courts ruled in these women's favor and, if they did, they were struck down on a higher level of the justice system both in Japan and in the United States.

This prompted intensification of civil society activity. One of the most important of such actions was a demonstration that has taken place every Wednesday in front of Japan's embassy in Seoul, Korea beginning on January 8, 1992. The Korean Council for the Women Drafted for Military Sexual Slavery by Japan (the Korean Council) has led these demonstrations. The Korean Council is the principal Korean civil society organization (CSO) dedicated to addressing the comfort women issue. The Korean Council's demonstrations have called upon the government of Japan to admit its official role in the creation and implementation of the system and to accept responsibility. The Korean Council has demanded that the Japanese government offer official compensation to survivors, take legal action against any surviving Japanese officials who helped to organize and implement the comfort women system, and also agree to teach about this shameful chapter of national history that destroyed the lives of tens of thousands of women in the official textbooks used in Japanese schools as a way to condemn and discourage such actions from ever recurring in the future.

For decades, most Japanese maintained their reserved demeanor on this topic with inimitable Japanese politeness. Most Japanese, after all, had a different understanding of this chapter of history than Koreans had. The Japanese had been taught the official Japanese account of historical events – that the comfort women had acted voluntarily as professional prostitutes servicing the military. They had been treated and compensated well for their work and were portrayed as having fulfilled a patriotic duty.[1]

The Korean Council persevered with its understanding of events, using a

---

[1] C. Sarah Soh, *The Comfort Women: Sexual Violence and Postcolonial Memory in Korea and Japan* (Chicago: University of Chicago Press, 2008), 71.

growing volume of evidence uncovered in previously inaccessible government archives in Japan and the United States. The Korean Council's supporters also successfully lobbied for the appointment in 1994 of a special rapporteur to the United Nations Human Rights Commission to investigate the comfort women issue. In 1999 the findings of this extensive UN investigation led to a sharp rebuke of Japan for having engaged in massive violations of women's rights. The year 2007 even saw the passage of a non-binding resolution by the United States House of Representatives calling upon Japan to recognize its culpability.

Yet the acts most impactful on Japan's demeanor on this topic were not based on investigations or legislation. On the occasion of its 1000th Wednesday demonstration on December 14, 2011, the Korean Council erected the statue of a comfort woman directly across from the Japanese embassy in Seoul. The Japanese abandoned their reserved demeanor. They condemned this action and launched a formal protest against Korea, arguing that the statue impaired Japan's dignity and constituted a violation of guidelines and protocols that a host country should follow when welcoming an embassy from a member of the community of nations with which it engages in diplomatic relations.[2]

The first memorial to provoke an official response from Japan was created in 2010 not in Seoul but on the grounds of the Palisades Park Municipal Library in New Jersey. Although Palisades Park represents a community of only 20,000, more than half of whom are of Korean heritage, this symbolic act led to formal visits to the office of the mayor, both by the Japanese Consulate in New York and by members of the Japanese Diet (Japan's parliament). Diet members challenged the historical accuracy and fairness of the allegations that the comfort women system represented a crime against humanity. Without effect, they argued that the women had been volunteers who were well compensated.[3] In establishing a memorial in Palisades Park and in erecting a statue in front of the embassy of Japan, Koreans, intentionally or not, had established powerful leverage that helped to bring a Japan, which famously cringes at humiliation, to the bargaining table.

Still today, every time a new statue or memorial is erected, whether in Korea, the United States, or Europe, it embarrasses Japan. It provides one additional point of leverage for the Korean Council and other CSOs which call upon

---

[2] *Vienna Convention on Diplomatic Relations*, Vienna, April 18, 1961, *United Nations Treaty Series*, vol. 500, http://legal.un.org/ilc/texts/instruments/english/conventions/9_1_1961.pdf, emphasis added.

[3] *Vienna Convention on Diplomatic Relations*, Vienna, April 18, 1961, *United Nations Treaty Series*, vol. 500.

Japan to accept responsibility and resolve the problem. For Korea, the problem is about justice for the comfort women and restoration of Korea's dignity as a nation. For Japan, the problem is about what they view as unfair national humiliation and a significant loss of "face." In either case, we should be clear that at this stage, the Korean Council, whether the problem is resolved or not, has no intention of seeing the statues come down. The statues and memorials may have never been erected if the problem had been solved earlier, but, now that they are in place, they are thought to represent an important piece of history.

The Ongoing Proliferation of Comfort Women Memorials in the United States

At least a dozen memorials have been established in the United States with a few statues remaining in mothballs, waiting for a permanent home in a park or in some other prominent venue in the town or city where Koreans attempt to erect them. Comfort women memorials have been set up in New Jersey, New York, Virginia, Maryland, Michigan, Texas, Georgia, and California. New Jersey, New York, and California each have three.

The highest profile memorial in the United States is the memorial established in Glendale, California, with the support of the Korean-American Forum of California. It is an exact replica of the statue near the Japanese embassy in Seoul. The Glendale statue resulted in lawsuits and, as in the case of exhibits in New York, New Jersey, and Virginia, led to formal protests from the government of Japan. The memorials stir sharp reactions from Japan because they universally state in their inscriptions that the women were *abducted* by the Japanese military, even though, based on their testimonies, most Korean and Taiwanese women have explained that they were lured by false promises of education and careers in fields such as nursing, food services, entertainment, and clerical work. They also point to the memorial's assertion that there were "more than 200,000" comfort women. In this text we clarify that the estimates set by fair-minded researchers, who have reviewed archival evidence on the comfort stations and Japanese troop deployments and also heard and examined testimonies from the comfort women and from the Japanese military who have come forward, is between 50,000 and 200,000.

2

The Origins and Implementation of the Comfort Women System

The term "comfort woman" ("慰安婦" pronounced *ianfu* in Japanese, *wianbu* in Korean and *Wèi'ān fù* in Mandarin), literally means "comforting, consoling woman" and is a euphemistic way of referring to those women conscripted by Japan during WWII to provide sexual services for the Japanese military. The term has a long history, tracing back to the 15th century reign of King Sejong in Korea.[1] The comfort women are nonetheless frequently referred to as "sex slaves" or "sexual slaves" in Korea and in the United States by the main Korean and Korean-American CSOs who have championed the comfort women cause. Such groups have lobbied for government resolutions for the vindication of the comfort women among other efforts. More recently they have also sought government support for the erection of dozens of comfort women memorials in the United States.

The Japanese government and one Japanese and Japanese-American CSO, the Global Alliance for Historical Truth (GAHT), also normally refer to the victims as "comfort women." However, they have also described the comfort women as "prostitutes," in response to the allegations of sexual slavery by Korean and Korean-American CSOs supporting the comfort women cause.[2] Dr. Koichi Mera, the founder of GAHT, normally uses the term "comfort women," opposes the Korean narrative on the comfort women, and has taken the position that prostitution can be an honorable career choice for those facing poverty.[3] In this text, in the hopes of conveying the greatest respect to the victims of this tragedy, we use the term "comfort women." We also use the

---

[1] Soh, *The Comfort Women*, 232.
[2] "Koichi Mera: President of GAHT-US Corporation (GAHT: the Global Alliance for Historical Truth)," YouTube video, press conference with Koichi Mera, posted by "The Foreign Correspondents' Club of Japan," August 25, 2016, https://www.youtube.com/watch?v=JkkS5AhdKeY.
[3] "Koichi Mera: President of GAHT-US Corporation (GAHT: the Global Alliance for Historical Truth)," YouTube video.

term "comfort women" for those recruited by Japan's provisional post-WWII government to provide sex for U.S. GIs between August 1945 and March 1946, at which time the operations were closed by order of General Douglas MacArthur, Supreme Commander of the Allied Powers (SCAP).

The Rationale for the Creation of the Comfort Women System

The official reasons usually given for the creation of the comfort women system and the conscripting of Korean and Taiwanese women into it are:

1. To prevent the rape of women in territory newly occupied by Japanese military forces, particularly following the atrocities surrounding the 1937 Nanjing Massacre. The large-scale raping of women by the Japanese military had occurred when Japan expanded its network of influence in Manchukuo, Nanjing, Shanghai, and beyond. [4]

2. To prevent the spread of sexually transmitted diseases (STDs) among the Japanese military forces. [5]

With the expansion of Japan's military presence in the 1930s, the perceived need for comfort stations increased. After 1937 Japan relied increasingly on women who were not Japanese. Koreans were the first to be conscripted into the new system. Japanese women remained available to Japan's commissioned officers but even commissioned officers often preferred the Korean women who were often younger and less experienced than the professional Japanese prostitutes used at that time.[6] One reason for the conscripting of non-Japanese into the system stemmed from concern among leaders that the Japanese military would be demoralized were they to discover their own sisters and wives among those mobilized as sex workers for the military.[7]

Unlike Chinese and Malaysians, Korean and Taiwanese women were Japanese subjects. The majority of Taiwanese and Korean comfort women also spoke Japanese and understood Japanese culture. The military

---
[4] Yuki Tanaka, *Japan's Comfort Women: Sexual Slavery and Prostitution during World War II and the US Occupation* (New York: Routledge, 2002), 45, 60.
[5] Tanaka, *Japan's Comfort Women: Sexual Slavery and Prostitution during World War II and the US Occupation*, 47, 60.
[6] Tanaka, *Japan's Comfort Women: Sexual Slavery and Prostitution during World War II and the US Occupation*, 90.
[7] Yoshiaki Yoshimi, *Comfort Women: Sexual Slavery in the Japanese Military during WWII* (New York: Columbia University Press, 2002), 155.

assumed that they had a certain loyalty to Japan.

The Comfort Women's Tribulations

A Korean woman or girl who responded to an ad to work in an office, as a nurse, a restaurant server, or even an entertainer rarely had any idea of what awaited her when she arrived at a military camp in the Pacific War theater. Upon arrival, these women and girls were introduced to a routine where they were coerced into having multiple sexual encounters daily, even several each hour in some cases. Japan's military medical corps closely monitored these women through check-ups to detect STDs.[8] Military doctors and medical workers frequently raped the women during these examinations.[9] The comfort women felt threatened and were forced to perform sexually on a daily basis, even during their menstrual cycle. Their military "johns" could punish them if they left a session unsatisfied. When women resisted having sex, they could be sharply disciplined through various means, including severe beatings.[10] Because they serviced troops along the Japanese Imperial Army's frontlines, many comfort women perished as Allied forces overwhelmed Japan's Pacific defense and annihilated Japan's troop encampments.[11] In the Battle of Saipan, comfort women, along with many other Japanese soldiers and civilians, reportedly chose suicide rather than surrender to the Allied forces.[12] In certain cases, the Japanese military also executed the Korean comfort women when they retreated from losing battles with Allied forces.[13]

Determining the Number of Women Conscripted into the Comfort Women System

Debate exists on the total number of comfort women who came from Korea, Taiwan, and Japan. The estimate of between 170,000 and 200,000 is attributed to Kim Il Myon, an early researcher of the comfort women in 1976.[14]

---

[8] Yoshimi, *Comfort Women: Sexual Slavery in the Japanese Military during WWII*.
[9] US Congress, House of Representatives, Subcommittee on Asia, the Pacific, and the Global Environment Committee on Foreign Affairs, *Hearing on Protecting the Human Rights of "Comfort Women,"* Statement by Jan Ruff O'Herne AO Friends of "Comfort Women" in Australia, February 15, 2007, https://web.archive.org/web/20070228195049/http://foreignaffairs.house.gov/110/ohe021507.htm
[10] Yoshiaki, *Comfort Women*, 151.
[11] George Hicks, *The Comfort Women: Japan's Brutal Regime of Enforced Prostitution in the Second World War* (New York: W. W. Norton & Company, 1995), 153-155.
[12] Nancy Bartlit, "Japanese Mass Suicides," Atomic Heritage Foundation, July 28, 2016, http://www.atomicheritage.org/history/japanese-mass-suicides.
[13] Hicks, *The Comfort Women*, 154.
[14] "Number of Comfort Stations and Comfort Women," Asian Women's Fund, http://awf.or.jp/e1/facts-07.html.

Kim's sources have been challenged by the Asian Women's Fund, an organization developed by Japan to offer symbolic compensation to victims and frame an official Japanese narrative, because they are attributed to parts of a speech delivered in 1965 by Japanese Diet Member Arafune Seijuro. Arafune specialized in hyperbole; he allegedly told an audience of supporters that Koreans claimed that 142,000 Korean comfort women had died during the Asia-Pacific War because of sexual abuses committed by the Japanese military and that Koreans claimed that 576,000 Korean soldiers had died in the war[15] – a number far higher than the 209,000 Koreans estimated to have served as combatants in the Japanese military.[16] A total of 192 Korean women have self-identified and been confirmed as "comfort women."[17]

Japanese historian Ikuhiko Hata initially estimated the total number of comfort women at approximately 90,000 but has since reduced that figure to 20,000. Some feel that he reduced this number for political reasons. Japanese historian Dr. Yoshimi Yoshiaki, credited with uncovering the first documented evidence that confirmed the system's existence in the early 1990s, estimates the number at between 50,000 and 200,000.[18] Credible academic researchers usually point to Yoshiaki's figure as the most probable range of the numbers of women involved.[19] This number again contrasts with the inscriptions on monuments in the United States including those in New Jersey, New York, Virginia, and California, which affirm the number of comfort women as "more than 200,000."[20] Nevertheless, it is clear that many tens of thousands of women were victimized by the system.

Methods of Recruitment

Most Korean women were deceptively recruited into the system by promises of careers in nursing, clerical work, or restaurants only to find themselves coerced into becoming sex providers.[21] In some cases, impoverished Korean families sold their daughters.[22] Research shows that, on rare occasions,

---

[15] "The 'Comfort Women' Issue and the Asian Women's Fund," Asian Women's Fund, 12, http://www.awf.or.jp/pdf/0170.pdf.
[16] Brian Palmer, *Fighting for the Enemy: Koreans in Japan's War 1937-1945* (Seattle: University of Washington Press, 2013), 123.
[17] "7. How Have the Women Lived after the War?, " Fight for Justice, http://fightforjustice.info/?page_id=2772&lang=en.
[18] "Number of Comfort Stations," Asian Women's Fund
[19] Tanaka, *Japan's Comfort Women*, 140-141.
[20] Kirk Semple, "In New Jersey, Memorial for 'Comfort Women' Deepens Old Animosity," *New York Times,* May 18, 2012, http://www.nytimes.com/2012/05/19/nyregion/monument-in-palisades-park-nj-irritates-japanese-officials.html.
[21] Tanaka, *Japan's Comfort Women*, 42.
[22] Tanaka, *Japan's Comfort Women*, 42-43.

Japanese soldiers also pillaged Korean villages and took young mothers and teenage girls with them.[23] The memorials established in the United States assert that the Japanese military abducted all the comfort women. However, that was not the norm for the women conscripted into the system from Japan, Korea, and Taiwan.

The Japanese women who joined the military comfort stations were largely professional prostitutes.[24] In the case of Taiwan and Korea, the comfort women were not professional prostitutes. They were largely young women who were deceived by brokers, often Korean or Taiwanese, acting on behalf of the Japanese military. Dr. Chu Te-lan, a recognized authority on Taiwan's comfort women, interviewed almost all of the fifty-eight Taiwanese women who self-identified as "comfort women" in the 1990s in Taiwan. She found that only three of the women interviewed understood ahead of time that they would be serving as sex workers.[25] In the case of Taiwan, some women had actually served as nurses prior to their conscription as comfort women and had agreed to serve as nurses for the Japanese military but instead faced a different fate.[26] As mentioned previously, Koreans were also deceived with the same empty promises of jobs as restaurant servers, entertainers, office workers, and even the promise of opportunities to further their education, only to find themselves reduced to being exploited and coerced into becoming comfort women.[27]

Official versus Ad Hoc Recruitment of Comfort Women

There are two distinct types of "comfort women." One group consisted of women who were recruited and conscripted by, or with the support of, the highest levels of the Japanese military and other branches of the Japanese government including the Ministry of Foreign Affairs. The Home Ministry was also engaged in operations to move comfort women discreetly from Japan, Korea, and Taiwan to mainland China and to key battlefronts of the Pacific War.[28]

---

[23] Although the Japanese dispute that women were taken in this way, Korean allegations to this effect are supported by the graphic description of rape and sequestration that Filipinas suffered in the creation of comfort women stations in the Philippines. See also Tanaka, *Japan's Comfort Women*, 49. However, both Yoshiaki and Tanaka indicate that this was not the norm for Koreans.
[24] Tanaka, *Japan's Comfort Women*, 18.
[25] Dennis Halpin, "Taiwan's Comfort Women," The Point, December 30, 2016, http://newasiapolicypoint.blogspot.com/2016/12/taiwans-comfort-women.html.
[26] Tanaka, *Japan's Comfort Women*, 44.
[27] Tanaka, *Japan's Comfort Women*, 38–43.
[28] Yoshiaki, *Comfort Women*, 154–155.

The comfort women from Japan, Korea, and Taiwan were all subjects of the Japanese government. Because Korea and Taiwan were considered part of Japan, the Japanese, Korean, and Taiwanese comfort women were all viewed by the national government as fulfilling a patriotic duty in supporting Japan's war effort. Indeed, women, "for the good of the country," were "coaxed into providing sexual services to soldiers so as to help raise their morale and win the war."[29] The Japanese government trusted Koreans and Taiwanese far more than other non-Japanese ethnic groups. Many of them perished with soldiers on the battlefields in the final days of the war.

The second group of comfort women were officially overseen by Japan's Ministry of Defense. Such women were abducted or otherwise conscripted onsite on an *ad hoc* basis by Japanese military units stationed in occupied territories. These women were not subjects of Japan (i.e., Korean, Taiwanese, or Japanese), and, rather than being perceived as performing a patriotic duty, they represented and were treated as "spoils of war." The Japanese commanding military officer in a certain area could order the procurement of local women to serve as comfort women. Most Filipina, Indonesian, Malaysian, Dutch, and Chinese women were brought into the comfort women system under these conditions. These women endured dehumanizing conditions and were likely treated even worse than the Japanese, Korean, and Taiwanese comfort women because they were not viewed as part of the Empire but as Japan's mortal enemies who were thus expendable. Dr. Koichi Mera of GAHT does not deny that abductions and mistreatment happened in the cases of the Filipinas, the Chinese, or the Indonesians who did not hold Japanese citizenship.[30]

The "Special Status" Attributed to Koreans and Taiwanese

Following China's defeat in the Sino-Japanese War, China ceded control of Taiwan to Japan through the 1895 Treaty of Shimonoseki. Japan's victory in the Russo-Japanese War also gave Japan supremacy on the Korean peninsula. Japan pressured Korea to accept the Eulsa Treaty of 1905, by which Japan agreed to "maintain the welfare and dignity of the Imperial House of Korea" until the time "when it is recognized that Korea has attained national strength."[31] This empty assurance effectively served as the rationale to annex Korea into the Japanese Empire.

As it built its Western-style empire in the 1930s, Japanese distinguished

---

[29] Soh, *The Comfort Women*, 71.
[30] "Koichi Mera: President of GAHT-US," Youtube video.
[31] Ministry of Foreign Affairs of the Republic of Korea, "The Eulsa Restriction Treaty," November 17, 1905, http://dokdo.mofa.go.kr/m/eng/pds/pomflet_03.jsp.

between those from the *gaichi* (outer lands) and from the *naichi* (the homeland). Nevertheless, as WWII proceeded, Japan increasingly recognized that it needed the support of both the *naichi* and the *gaichi* in the war effort. In 1942 Korea and Taiwan were both placed under the authority of the Office of Home Affairs, sending the clear signal that Koreans and Taiwanese alike were being regarded as Japanese nationals.[32] In the final year of the war, Koreans and Taiwanese were also made eligible for military conscription. Koreans and Taiwanese were also encouraged if not pressured to take on Japanese names. Members of Korea's royal family were encouraged to marry with Japanese royalty.

The policies of Japan toward Korea were not genocidal in their intent. Japan's policies sharply contrasted with the policies of Nazi Germany towards the Jews. Nazi Germany clearly sought the annihilation of the Jews.[33] If Germans intermarried with Jews, the offspring of such a mixed marriage were automatically classified as Jewish. The camps of Dachau, Buchenwald, and Auschwitz awaited the children, the Jewish spouse, and possibly the impudent German who had consciously married a Jew. In contrast, Japan sought to assimilate rather than eradicate Koreans and Taiwanese.

Korean supporters of comfort women memorials often seek to draw parallels between the fate of Korean comfort women and the Jewish Holocaust.[34] *Korea Times* chief Editor Oh Young-jin even admitted that he sought to "to make the Koreans out like the Jews" and get people to "see Korea's misery as compelling as they see the Jewish Holocaust" to gain support for Korea.[35] Nevertheless, evidence is manifest that Japan had no intention or grand scheme to eliminate Koreans, even though they clearly wished to eradicate the Korean national identity.

Asian Culture as a Facilitator of the Comfort Woman System

C. Sarah Soh's *Comfort Women: Sexual Violence and Postcolonial Memory*

---

[32] Ching-chih Chen, *The Japanese Colonial Empire, 1895–1945*, ed. Ramon Hawley Myers and Mark Peattie (Princeton: Princeton University Press, 1984), 243.
[33] "Hitler Talks of Jewish 'Annihilation,' " WW2 History, \http://ww2history.com/key_moments/Holocaust/Hitler_talks_of_Jewish_annihilation.
[34] See, e.g., Antonio Olivo, "Memorial to WWII Comfort Women Dedicated in Fairfax County amid Protests," *Washington Post,* May 30, 2014, \https://www.washingtonpost.com/local/memorial-to-wwii-comfort-women-dedicated-in-fairfax-county/2014/05/30/730a1248-e684-11e3-a86b-362fd5443d19_story.html?utm_term=.9de22c4bdfb0.
[35] Oh Young-jin, "Holocaust vs. Comfort Women," *The Korea Times,* June 2, 2017, http://www.koreatimes.co.kr/www/opinion/2017/06/667_230509.html.

in Korea and Japan (2008) represents one of the few studies on comfort women that offers insights into the social conditions and prevalent attitudes that led to the creation of the comfort women system. Soh looks not just at Japan's but also Korea's patriarchal views which, she asserts, enabled the system's creation and its continuation with some permutations beyond WWII. Soh describes herself as "a supporter of the transnational feminist movement" and explains that she wrote her book on the comfort women to "transcend the ethnonationalist politics of 'partial truths' by presenting a complicated picture that may disrupt the currently internationalized normative though partial and partisan understandings of the Korean comfort women's horrific experience."[36]

The Forerunner of Japan's Military Comfort Women System

In the fifteen-year period following the 1853 arrival of U.S. Commodore Matthew Perry in Japan, Japan's Tokugawa Shogunate weakened and finally collapsed. The emperor assumed leadership of the nation and stood as the center of both religious and political power, replacing the military rule of the Tokugawa Shogunate. With the initiation of the Meiji Empire, governance of the state largely shifted to the samurai civil servant class who led Japan's transformation from a feudal power to an industrialized, modern state. To avoid the fate that China suffered at the hands of the West, Japan chose to open to trade with the West rather than resist. Japan decided to learn from the West's successes rather than remain isolated.

Based on its study of the West, the Meiji Empire in the late nineteenth century worked to establish democratic institutions, industrialize, and evolve into a modern military power. Japan's leaders concluded that central to the West's success was its creation of an overseas imperial presence. Japan, they concluded, also needed to become an imperial power. They planned to advance their imperial ambitions through promoting what came to be known as the Greater East Asia Co-Prosperity Sphere, Japan's rendition of a European style colonial empire.

In its rise to power and its bid to become the principal Pacific hegemon, Japan fought wars with China (1894–95) and Russia (1904–05). Japan prevailed in both of these wars. As discussed previously, the Sino-Japanese War led to Japan acquiring Taiwan and the Russo-Japanese War resulted in Japan gaining hegemony over Korea. Japan then proceeded to make strides toward establishing itself on the Chinese mainland, starting with Manchuria where it eventually established its puppet state of Manchukuo. It consolidated its newly acquired network of commerce and trade through the deployment of military forces in the newly established colonies of Taiwan and Korea and its

---

[36] Soh, The Comfort Women, xvii.

client states beginning with Manchukuo.

Japan's practice of exporting indentured Japanese sex workers overseas was in place by the latter part of the nineteenth century.[37] As Japan expanded territorially, the leadership considered that its overseas merchants and its military forces needed female companionship. Japanese professional prostitutes, frequently referred to as "karayuki-san" (translated as "China-going persons") were dispatched from Japan to serve as sex workers.[38]

The karayuki-san provided temporary companionship and sexual favors for the overseas Japanese military and the businessmen and traders who accompanied them. The original karayuki-san of the nineteen century were Japanese in origin and ethnicity.[39] By 1910 there were 47,541 such prostitutes in Japan and an additional 19,000 Japanese sex workers in Russia, China, Hong Kong, Singapore, and other parts of Southeast Asia.[40] Japanese prostitutes, unlike their Chinese and Russian counterparts, readily made their services available to non-Japanese clients. In 1918 Japanese government policy changed, however, and Japanese *karayuki-san* were required to limit offering their services to Japanese citizens.[41] Noting parallels between the *karayuki-san* system and the comfort women system, research scholar Yuki Tanaka makes the following observation:

> The *karayuki-san* system was undoubtedly a repressive system of sexual exploitation. The methods of procuring young women were clearly unlawful and morally unjustifiable. In this sense, they were little different from the methods that were used for the later procurement of comfort women. In both cases serious criminal acts were involved.[42]

Tanaka points out that many of the *karayuki-san* of poor family background in Nagasaki were sold by their parents to procurers and then sent to various places in the Asia-Pacific region.[43] From 1922 onward, the Japanese *karayuki-san* in China began to be supplemented by Korean women.[44] In the pre-war period, many of these women were, for all practical purposes, indentured servants if not slaves. According to Tanaka, the women were

---

[37] Tanaka, *Japan's Comfort Women*, 167-173.
[38] Tanaka, *Japan's Comfort Women*, 167.
[39] Tanaka, *Japan's Comfort Women*, 168–169.
[40] Tanaka, *Japan's Comfort Women*, 169.
[41] Tanaka, *Japan's Comfort Women*, 172.
[42] Tanaka, *Japan's Comfort Women*, 173.
[43] Tanaka, *Japan's Comfort Women*, 10.
[44] Tanaka, *Japan's Comfort Women*, 36–37.

"purchased" for between $500 and $600 and were required to reimburse their "sponsors" if they were ever to return home.[45]

The protocols in place for the *karayuki-san* and the WWII comfort women were in many ways similar. Whenever they engaged a client, the *kayayuki-san*, just like the WWII comfort women, received a ticket, indicating that a payment had been made. Approximately 50% of the fee for this ticket went to the *karayuki-san*.[46] Although the "comfort women" were theoretically also to receive a portion of the fee paid for their time and services, that was often not the case because of alleged debts that the comfort women were expected to amortize and because of injustices and graft within the system itself.[47]

The original exclusively Japanese *karayuki-san* staffed sex industry proved to be a lucrative source of foreign reserves for Japan. The *karayuki-sans'* earnings often returned as remittances to Japan to help to support the *karayuki-sans'* Japan-based families. Tanaka cites the case of Dalian in China where, in 1900, $630,000 of the $1,000,000 in remittances sent back to Japan originated from the sex industry.[48] Tanaka describes the working conditions of the "*karayuki-san*" as follows:

> Each woman was sold to a brothel for between $500 and $600, which was levied upon her as a "debt" by her brothel keeper. Even in the case of kidnappings, a levy was imposed for "travel expenses." As a result almost all *karayuki-san* were financially bound to their brothels for years until this "debt" was paid off.[49]

Tanaka's research shows that debt, sickness, and despair "drove many *karayuki-san* to suicide." For Tanaka, "it is indisputable that the comfort women system was essentially based on the *karayuki-san* system."[50] C. Sarah Soh, nevertheless, points out that three major differences existed between the *karayuki-san* and those conscripted into the comfort women system:

> 1. *Ianfu* were only available to the military while the *karayuki-san* had a broader clientele; 2. The *Ianjo* or comfort stations were managed by the Japanese military; 3. *Ianfu*, many of

---

[45] Tanaka, *Japan's Comfort Women*, 170.
[46] Tanaka, *Japan's Comfort Women*.
[47] Yoshiaki, *Comfort Women*, 142–144.
[48] Tanaka, *Japan's Comfort Women*, 170.
[49] Tanaka, *Japan's Comfort Women*.
[50] Tanaka, *Japan's Comfort Women*.

whom were not ethnically Japanese, faced more violent attacks than the *karayuki-san* who were.[51]

The Beginning of Japan's Military Comfort Women System

Japan's military supported a massive influx of comfort women to reduce the risk of women being raped in areas newly occupied by Japan's military. As noted, they also established the comfort stations to prevent the spread of sexually transmitted disease.[52] Tanaka points out that "in December 1937, the Central China Area Army issued an instruction to each contingent force to set up comfort stations."[53] However, as the war effort with China intensified, Japan decided against a mass mobilization of Japanese women to overseas military brothels.

To avoid negatively impacting its military's morale through soldiers seeing Japanese women, even relatives, conscripted into the comfort women system,[54] Japan turned instead to its colonies, deploying hundreds of Korean women by January 1938[55] followed within a few months by a "full scale mobilization" of Koreans.[56] Taiwanese were drafted into Japan's war efforts beginning in 1937 under Japan's national mobilization policy;[57] Taiwanese comfort women researchers and activists point to 1938 as the first year that Taiwanese women were mobilized as military comfort women.[58]

Japan made a conscientious effort to upgrade the status and public appreciation of comfort women. One Japanese medical doctor in Manchuria described a cohort of comfort women as "a military force itself" and "therefore not just prostitutes."[59] In Japan, comfort women were promised that, based on their service, they would be enshrined at the Japanese national military memorial shrine, Yasukuni, as "servers of the nation."[60]

---

[51] Soh, *The Comfort Women*, 115.
[52] Soh, *The Comfort Women*, 10.
[53] Soh, *The Comfort Women*, 18.
[54] Yoshiaki, *Comfort Women*, 155.
[55] Tanaka, *Japan's Comfort Women*, 52–54.
[56] Tanaka, *Japan's Comfort Women*, 14.
[57] Soh, *The Comfort Women*, 62.
[58] Graceia Lai, Wu Hui-Ling, and Yu Ju-Fen, *Silent Scars: History of Sexual Slavery by the Japanese Military: A Pictorial Book*, trans. Shing-mei Ma (Taipei: Taipei Women's Rescue Foundation, 2005), 74.
[59] Tanaka, *Japan's Comfort Women*, 12.
[60] Haesel Kim, "Contending Narratives on the 'Comfort Women' Issue in Japan and South Korea" (paper, Colgate University), 13, http://www.colgate.edu/docs/default-source/default-document-library/kim-lampert-paper-2016.pdf.

The Japanese government also made patriotic appeals to its colonies. Gary Marvin Davison in *A Short History of Taiwan* confirms that many Taiwanese "embraced the Japanese vision of a united Greater East Asia and looked forward to rising citizenship status within the empire."[61] Dr. Chu Te-lan, a senior researcher in Academia Sinica's Research Center for the Humanities and Social Sciences and a recognized authority on Taiwan's comfort women, reminds her readers that Japan's war effort was portrayed as a "Holy (Just) War" to end European rule and assure that "Asia be for Asians."[62] Even when brought to overseas military camps on false pretenses, Taiwanese women were coerced to provide sexual services to the Japanese military "in the name of patriotism to the country."[63] C. Sarah Soh points out that Korean women were also asked to serve as comfort women once they arrived overseas and to view this as a patriotic act.[64] Today in Taiwan, pro-Japan extremists continue to spark controversy by claiming that becoming a comfort woman represented "moving upward."[65]

The Fate of Comfort Women Following World War II

Upon returning to Korea, the suffering of the comfort women continued. Female promiscuity was taboo in Korean society, which attributed great value to premarital virginity. The loss of a Korean woman's virginity, even under the horrible circumstances of the comfort women system, meant that the survivors of the system had little or no chance of ever marrying. In a February 1994 complaint filed with the Office of Chief Prosecutor of Tokyo, the Korean Council for the Women Drafted for Military Sexual Slavery by Japan (the Korean Council) detailed the post-war hardships experienced by 19 comfort women. The Korean Council's findings indicated that if the former comfort women married, their marriages typically failed. Fifty years after the end of the war, 15 of the 19 comfort women included in the study were found to be "living alone" with no child to take care of them.[66]

In December 1991 Kim Hak-Sun, a Korean, became the first woman to "go public" and identify herself as a former comfort woman. Just a few months later, in February 1992, Ms. Itoh Hideko, a former member of the Japan Diet,

---

[61] Gary Marvin Davison, *A Short History of Taiwan: The Case for Independence* (Westport, CT: Praeger, 2003), 75–76.
[62] Chu Te-lan (also romanized Zhu Delan), "太平洋戰爭與臺灣原住民「慰安婦」(1941–1945)" 近代中國 163, (2005): 58–60.
[63] Lai et al., *Silent Scars*, 87.
[64] Soh, *The Comfort Women,* 71.
[65] Lai et al., *Silent Scars,* 119.
[66] See legal complaint by the Korean Council for the Women Drafted for Military Sexual Slavery by Japan to the Chief Prosecutor Tokyo District Prosecutors' Office in February 7, 1994, http://www.vcn.bc.ca/alpha/learn/comp.htm.

uncovered three telegrams in the Japanese Defense Agency that confirmed that not just Koreans but also Taiwanese women had been dispatched as comfort women. The telegrams referenced a March 12, 1942 request for 50 women to be sent to Borneo from Taiwan. A later telegram requested an additional 20 women because the women were overworked and exhausted. The telegrams confirmed "beyond doubt that during WWII, Taiwanese women were sent to the Japanese frontline as sexual slaves for the Japanese Military."[67]

In the months following Itoh's uncovering of the telegrams, the first Taiwanese came forward identifying themselves as "comfort women." Like many of the Korean comfort women, the Taiwanese were initially reticent about identifying themselves in public: "veiled behind black drapes, they accused the Japanese government, reclaiming their dignity, seeking an apology and reparations."[68] In most cases, their testimonies showed that the young Taiwanese women who joined Japan's military effort, not understanding that they would become comfort women, did so at their parents' behest. In some cases, they joined on their own accord but even then it was done with the intention of helping their families.

A few Taiwanese comfort women said that they had actually been sold by their families to Taiwanese brothels and from there were sent to comfort stations abroad.[69] Most Taiwanese comfort women who were interviewed had been born to impoverished families, and their parents worked as peasant farmers, fishermen, laborers, and street vendors.[70] Nevertheless, some women from well-to-do Taiwanese families also apparently ended up being deceptively recruited into the system. When interviewed, one Taiwanese comfort woman reflected on a co-worker named Mitsue whom she described as well-read and with excellent calligraphy. She pondered how her friend could be "so unlucky as to be tricked to come here?"[71] A nurse who had been recruited recalled how, on the first day, she and her fellow nurses realized they "were cheated" and she wept: "I was nineteen, with a wonderful prospect in life. And now, my youth, my virginity, and my dignity were all buried at this comfort station."[72]

When interviewed, one Taiwanese comfort woman reflected on how she was

---

[67] Lai et al., *Silent Scars*, 73–74.
[68] Lai et al., *Silent Scars*, 78.
[69] Chu Te-lan (also romanized as Zhu Delan), "Taiwan 'ianfu' mondai: ronsô to kenkyû," *Rekishigaku kenkyû*, no. 849 (2001).
[70] Lai et al., *Silent Scars*, 76.
[71] Lai et al., *Silent Scars*, 55–56.
[72] Lai et al., *Silent Scars*, 56.

confronted on the first day by the harsh orders of a Japanese woman: "once you are here, you'd better listen and do what I say." The interviewee was unsuccessful in three attempts to commit suicide "by drinking antiseptic" and so she "continued to be assaulted." When she returned home after the war, her uncle admonished her, saying "our family can't have whores." When she finally married, she was unable to bear children, and her mother-in-law forced her to accept divorce. She made her living by selling coconuts and added, "I often drink alone, cup after cup, to forget about my pain."[73] Another of those interviewed lamented, **"**I used to be a clean girl but I was trashed by the Japanese." Filled with guilt, she regularly visited a temple seeking "mercy from the Goddess of Mercy." Emphatic that she was "forced" and clear that the guilt resides with those who took advantage of her, she nevertheless made it a habit to seek forgiveness: "I repent, eat vegetarian food, recite sutra, listen to sermons, and volunteer at the temple." Through this, she feels "better afterwards."[74]

---

[73] Lai et al., *Silent Scars,* 169.
[74] Lai et al., *Silent Scars,* 89.

3

Steps Toward Redress for the Comfort Women

The Five Decades of Silence

As Japan edged toward surrender, the Japanese government undertook a systematic destruction of documents to conceal war crimes including the creation and implementation of the repressive comfort women system.[1] In addition to destroying documents, the Japanese military disguised comfort women as Red Cross workers at the time of surrender so that they would not be identified as sex slaves.[2] The cover-up explains one of the key reasons why this matter remained hidden from the public's attention for almost half a century.

After Japan signed the Instrument of Surrender on September 2, 1945, ending WWII, the United States became the sole occupying power in Japan and took steps to prosecute Japanese war criminals. General Douglas MacArthur issued a decree on January 19, 1946, known as the Tokyo Charter, which set down the rules by which the Tokyo War Crimes Tribunal was to be conducted.

Although it was a unilateral decree rather than a treaty among the Allies, the Tokyo Charter was substantially the same as the Nuremberg Charter. Chief Prosecutor Joseph Keenan proposed a list of defendants to MacArthur. By MacArthur's decision, Emperor Hirohito was not subjected to prosecution. The focus of the prosecution was on "Class-A" crimes, which referred to a conspiracy to wage aggressive war. Class-B crimes involved the mistreatment of prisoners, and Class-C constituted crimes against humanity. Nothing was done at that time by the United States to investigate the comfort women

---

[1] Lai et al., *Silent Scars*, 49.
[2] Tanaka, *Japan's Comfort Women*, 81.

system or to hold anyone accountable for it.³

In 1948, however, the Batavia Military Tribunal did try 13 Japanese officers and comfort station operators for the forcible seizure for rape and prostitution of Dutch women living in Dutch Indonesia. The Dutch military court found seven officers and four civilian comfort station operators guilty.⁴ The names of both the victims and the accused were sealed but were acquired in 1992 by the Japanese newspaper *Asahi Shimbun* and published in detail.⁵ In sum, in the context of the intensifying Cold War, the Allied powers were most concerned with avenging the deaths of Allied soldiers, prisoners of war, and Dutch women, and did not investigate or prosecute the mistreatment of thousands of Asian women in the comfort women system.

The comfort women themselves remained in the shadows because of the deep shame and guilt that they felt as a result of their experiences. They did not wish to be further stigmatized but rather to live their lives quietly and as best as they could. It was only in 1991 that the first woman, Kim Hak Sun, came forward and publicly identified herself as a former comfort woman.

Korean Reaction to the Allies' Post-World War II Decision Not to Try the System's Perpetrators

Following annexation and throughout WWII, there is no evidence that the Korean independence movement ever raised concerns about the comfort women system and may very well have been unaware of its existence. Supporters of independence decried Japan's seizure of Koreans' food and property as well as the imposition of Shinto culture and the Japanese language. They also denounced Japan for subjecting Koreans to forced labor and the repression of the Korean independence movement. However, one does not find mention of the comfort women in the communications archives available in the Franklin Delano Roosevelt Presidential Library. Following the Japanese surrender in 1945 and the San Francisco Treaty of Peace in 1951, anti-Japan sentiment heightened in Korea. Korea's first president, Syngman Rhee, was staunchly anti-Japanese and opposed any easy path for restoring Korea-Japan relations that did not address Japan's deliberate intention and policy of annihilating the Korean culture and national identity. Only in 1965,

---

3   See Kathryn J. Witt, "Comfort Women: The 1946–1948 Tokyo War Crimes Trials and Historical Blindness," *Great Lakes Journal. Of Undergraduate History* 4, no. 1 (September 2016): 28–29.

4   Sue R. Lee, "Comforting the Comfort Women: Who Can Make Japan Pay?, " *University of Pennsylvania Journal of International Economic Law* 24, no. 2 (Summer 2003): 532.

5   Lee, "Comforting the Comfort Women: Who Can Make Japan Pay?, 533.

four years after the former Japanese army officer General Park Chung-hee seized power in Korea, did Japan and Korea establish formal diplomatic relations with each other.

Late in 1991, members of the Association of Korean Victims brought a claim to the Tokyo District Court. They alleged human rights violations during WWII against the Japanese government. The plaintiffs included three comfort women, including Kim Hak Sun. Other plaintiffs included 13 Korean men who contended that they had been forced to serve in the Japanese Imperial Army. The lawsuit alleged a sweeping range of abuses that Koreans had suffered during the period of Japan's "protection" without focusing on the comfort women. The comfort women co-plaintiffs sought "1) an official apology; 2) compensatory payment to survivors in lieu of full reparation – each plaintiff asked for ¥20 million ($154,000); 3) a thorough investigation of their cases; 4) the revision of Japanese school textbooks identifying this issue as part of the colonial oppression of the Korean people; and 5) the building of a memorial museum."[6]

The lawsuit was the first occasion on which Korean comfort women sought redress through the courts.[7] Their stories resonated broadly among Koreans, the international community, and women's rights organizations. Notably, they characterized the comfort women system as a "crime against humanity." They pointed to Japan's unconditional acceptance of the Potsdam and Cairo Declarations, which demanded, among other things, Korea's deliverance from a "condition of enslavement." The plaintiffs argued that this implied full restitution, and until that was made, the state of "enslavement" would still persist.[8] The Tokyo District Court dismissed the case in March 2001. Presiding Judge Shoichi Maruyama acknowledged the suffering of the plaintiffs but found that individual victims' claims for damages against the victimizer country were not cognizable under international law. Judge Maruyama further ruled that claims by individual South Koreans seeking compensation for wartime damages were precluded by the 1965 Treaty on Basic Relations between Japan and the Republic of Korea, which established basic domestic relations between the two countries,[9] and through the supplementary "Agreement on the Settlement of Problems Concerning Property and Claims and on Economic Cooperation," (the "1965 Economic Agreement") which specified that, through the indemnities paid at that time by Japan, all national and Korean citizen claims by Korea against Japan were

---

[6] "Memory and Reconciliation in the Asia-Pacific," George Washington University, http://www.gwu.edu/~memory/data/judic.
[7] Hicks, *The Comfort Women*, 11.
[8] Hicks, *The Comfort Women*, 200.
[9] "Memory and Reconciliation in the Asia-Pacific," George Washington University.

"settled completely and finally."[10]

The plaintiffs appealed to the Tokyo High Court which rejected their appeal in July 2003. Presiding Judge Sueo Kito stated that the Japanese government at the time had an obligation to protect the comfort women from danger, but the right to demand compensation had expired.[11] In November 2004, the Supreme Court upheld the Tokyo High Court's rule.[12]

In December 1992, former comfort women and other plaintiffs filed suit seeking a formal apology from Japan, to be made in the Japanese Diet and before the General Assembly of the United Nations, and damages totaling ¥286 million. This case gained traction when the Prefectural Court in Shiminoseki in April 1998 ruled in favor of the plaintiffs, finding that the Japanese Diet was legally obligated to enact a compensation law after the 1993 Kono Statement had accepted blame for the comfort women system.[13]

The Shimonoseki Court made extensive findings of fact with respect to the comfort women system. The Court found that,

> although private agents ran most of the comfort stations, in some regions, the Imperial Japanese forces directly managed the comfort stations. Even if private agents ran the comfort stations, the Japanese Imperial Forces influenced the management by setting the hours of operation, service fees, and regulations for the comfort station management. . . All of the 'Comfort Women' Plaintiffs were brought to the comfort stations through deception and forcefully turned into 'comfort women' by rape. The comfort stations had deep relations with the Imperial Japanese Forces.[14]

---

[10] *Agreement on the Settlement of Problems Concerning Property and Claims and on Economic Cooperation (with Protocols, Exchanges of Notes and Agreed Minutes)*, Tokyo, June 22, 1965, *United Nations Treaty Series* 583, no. 8473, https://treaties.un.org/doc/Publication/UNTS/Volume%20583/volume-583-I-8473-English.pdf.

[11] "Korean Comfort Women v. Japan," Memory Reconciliation, https://memoryreconciliation.org/topics/comfort-women/comfort-women-korea/.

[12] "Lawsuits Brought against Japan by Former Korean 'Comfort Women,' " Columbia Law School, http://www.law.columbia.edu/korean-legal-studies/sexual-slavery-during-wwi-comfort-women-issue/legal-documents-and-lawsuits/lawsuits-brought-former-korean-comfort-women.

[13] See Tahei Okada, trans., "The 'Comfort Women' Case: Judgment of April 27, 1998 Shimonseki Branch, Yamaguchi Prefectural Court, Japan," *Pacific Rim Law & Policy Journal* 8, no. 1 (January 1999): 63–108.

[14] Okada, trans., "The 'Comfort Women' Case: Judgment of April 27, 1998 Shimonseki Branch, Yamaguchi Prefectural Court, Japan," 5–8. At least one commentator noted

The Court ordered the Japanese government to pay ¥300,000 ($2,800) to each of three plaintiffs. The plaintiffs appealed to the Hiroshima High Court demanding a "proper apology and compensation" and claiming that the amount awarded them was an insult to their suffering.[15] In March 2001 the Hiroshima High Court rejected the appeal and reversed the lower court decision, saying that decisions regarding post-war compensation were the responsibility of the legislative branch, not the courts. The Supreme Court dismissed the subsequent appeal.[16]

By 1998 eight lawsuits had been filed in Japan but not one resulted in a final judgment in favor of the plaintiffs. The courts repeatedly found that the matter of wartime compensation settlements had been addressed through the San Francisco Peace Treaty of 1951 as well as the 1965 bilateral treaty and the associated Agreement between Japan and the Republic of Korea Concerning the Settlement of Problems in Regard to Property and Claims and Economic Cooperation.[17] Japan, the courts ruled, could thus not be held liable for additional compensation for these victims.

The American Legal System and the Comfort Women's Extension of Litigation to the United States

In September 2000, a group of 15 former comfort women (six Koreans, four Chinese, four Filipinos, and one Taiwanese) filed a class action lawsuit in the United States District Court for the District of Columbia under the Alien Tort Claims Act, a statute that permits foreigners to sue in U.S. courts for abuses of international law.[18] The U.S. government filed a statement of interest against the plaintiffs in the case, agreeing with Japan that the claims were barred by sovereign immunity and presented a non-justiciable political question. The District Court agreed on both grounds and dismissed the case in October 2001, adding that "this court is not the appropriate forum in which plaintiffs may seek to reopen . . . discussions [of war claims against Japan]

---

that the Shimonseki Court's findings of fact would aid political lobbying for resolution of the issue. See Etsuro Totsuka, trans., "Commentary on a Victory for 'Comfort Women': Japan's Judicial Recognition of Military Sexual Slavery," *Pacific Rim Law & Policy Journal* 8, no. 1 (January 1999): 47–61.

[15] "Lawsuits Brought against Japan," Colombia Law School.

[16] Miki Ishikida, "Lawsuits," sec. 3-2-4 in "The Comfort Women," chap. 3 in *Toward Peace: War Responsibility, Postwar Compensation, and Peace Movements and Education in Japan* (Bloomington: iUniverse, Inc., 2005; Center for US-Japan Comparative Social Studies, 2005), http://www.usjp.org/towardpeace_en/tpComfort_en.html#mozTocId298479.

[17] *Agreement on the Settlement of Problems, United Nations Treaty Series*.

[18] Hwang Geum Joo v. Japan, No. 00CV02233 (D.D.C. Sept. 18, 2000).

nearly a half century later."[19]

On June 27, 2003, the D.C. Circuit court affirmed the District Court's decision. The case was appealed to the U.S. Supreme Court, which vacated the judgment and remanded it to the Circuit Court for further consideration. The Circuit Court again dismissed the lawsuit in 2005, this time finding that it lacked jurisdiction under the political question doctrine. [20]

Although the court determined that it lacked jurisdiction, Chief Judge Douglas Ginsburg's opinion considered in some depth the legal effect of the 1951 Treaty of Peace between Japan and the Allied Powers and the subsequent 1965 Agreement between the Republic of Korea and Japan. The court noted that "it is pellucidly clear that the Allied Powers intended that all war-related claims against Japan be resolved through government-to-government negotiations rather than through private tort suits."[21] The court further observed that it is apparent and not contested by the plaintiffs that the "governments of the appellants' countries [had] the authority . . . to bargain away their private claims" and that this would be consistent with international law.[22] But ultimately, the Court ruled that adjudicating the plaintiffs' claims would require determining whether the post-war treaties signed by Japan foreclosed the private claims of wartime victims and that that question was a matter for the executive branch of the U.S. government to decide. The U.S. Supreme Court denied further review.[23]

In 2015, He Nam You and Kyung Soon Kim brought another class action suit against the government of Japan, Emperors Hirohito and Akihito, Prime Ministers Kishi and Abe, and multiple Japanese corporations and their U.S. subsidiaries for personal injuries sustained as comfort women during WWII.

---

[19] Hwang Geum Joo v. Japan, No. 00CV02233 (D.D.C. Sept. 18, 2000), and see Slip Op. at 23.
[20] Hwang Geum Joo v. Japan, 413 F.3d 45 (D.C. Cir. 2005).
[21] Hwang Geum Joo v. Japan, 413 F.3d 45 (D.C. Cir. 2005), 50.
[22] Hwang Geum Joo v. Japan, 413 F.3d 45 (D.C. Cir. 2005), citing Louis Henkin, Foreign Affairs and the Constitution 300 (2nd edition 1996) for the proposition that "governments have dealt with . . . private claims as their own, treating them as national assets, and as counters, 'chips', in international bargaining. Settlement agreements have lumped, or linked, claims deriving from private debts with others that were intergovernmental in origin, and concessions in regard to one category of claims might be set off against concessions in the other, or against larger political considerations unrelated to debts."
[23] See denial of certiorari in Hwang Geum Joo v. Japan, 546 U.S. 1208 (2006). See also "The Comfort Women Case: Supporting the Claims of WWII-Era Victims of Sexual Violence," The Center for Justice & Accountability, http://www.cja.org/article.php?id=328.

The case was ultimately dismissed on June 21, 2016 (without service on Japan, the Japanese corporations, or the individual defendants having been effectuated) on the grounds that the case, like the *Hwang* case, presented a non-justiciable political question; the court also ruled that the claims were time-barred and that plaintiffs had not demonstrated any basis to toll the running of the limitations period.[24]

The United Nations' Response to the Comfort Women Controversy

On March 4, 1994, the United Nations Commission on Human Rights adopted resolution 1994/45 in which it decided to appoint a special rapporteur on violence against women. Radhika Coomaraswamy, a Sri Lankan educated in the United States, was selected as the special rapporteur. As part of her mandate, Ms. Coomaraswamy visited South Korea and Japan gathering materials related to the comfort women issue and received additional materials from North Korea. She issued a report titled "Report of the Special Rapporteur on Violence against Women, Its Causes and Consequences" on February 5, 1996. She also issued an addendum to the report titled "Report on the Mission to the Democratic People's Republic of Korea, the Republic of Korea and Japan on the Issue of Military Sexual Slavery in Wartime" on January 4, 1996.[25]

The Coomaraswamy Report concluded that Japan had made widespread use of "sexual slavery" in the comfort women system and called on the government of Japan to acknowledge violations of international law and take legal responsibility, pay compensation to individual victims, make a public written apology, amend educational curricula, and identify and punish perpetrators.[26] The report also suggested that North Korea and South Korea might seek the involvement of the International Court of Justice.

The Coomaraswamy Report heavily invoked the now-debunked confessions of Seiji Yoshida. Ms. Coomaraswamy later found it necessary to clarify to H.E.

---

[24] You v. Japan, 2015 U.S. Dist. LEXIS 167129 (N.D. Cal. Dec. 14, 2015). See also You v. Japan, 2016 U.S. Dist. LEXIS 80699 (N.D. Cal. June 21, 2016).

[25] United Nations, Economic and Social Council, *Report on the Mission to the Democratic People's Republic of Korea, the Republic of Korea and Japan on the Issue of Military Sexual Slavery in Wartime*, E/CN.4/1996/53/Add.1 (January 4, 1996), http://www.un.org/Docs/journal/asp/ws.asp?m=E/CN.4/1996/53/Add.1. Commonly referred to as the *Coomaraswamy Report*.

[26] Notably, Ms. Coomaraswamy relied in part on the now-discredited confessions of Yoshida Seiji and the George Hicks book *Comfort Women: Sex Slaves of the Japanese Empire*, which also relied on Yoshida's confessions. See *Coomaraswamy Report* at 32–33, n. 1–11.

Kuni Sato, Japan's Ambassador for Human Rights, that she stood by the report's findings because Seiji Yoshida's testimony constituted only one part of a far broader body of evidence, and she maintained that the report's findings against Japan remained valid.[27]

In December 2000 the Violence Against Women in War-Network Japan organized a "People's Tribunal," the Women's International War Crimes Tribunal on Japan's Military Sexual Slavery, to conduct a mock criminal trial of Emperor Hirohito and other persons in connection with the comfort women system. The tribunal found the emperor guilty of rape and that the government of Japan had incurred state responsibility.[28]

---

[27] Mindy Kotler, "The Comfort Women and Japan's War on the Truth," *New York Times*, November 14, 2014, https://www.nytimes.com/2014/11/15/opinion/comfort-women-and-japans-war-on-truth.html?mcubz=1.

[28] See "Women's International War Crimes Tribunal 2000 for the Trial of Japanese Military Sexual Slavery," December 12, 2000, http://home.att.ne.jp/star/tribunal/jedgement-e.html.

4

Key Mileposts and Actors in Efforts to Settle the Ongoing Comfort Women Impasse

The Significance of the Treaty on Basic Relations between Japan and the Republic of Korea

When examining competing narratives regarding the comfort women system, it is important to have an awareness of key mileposts and actors in the efforts to find a settlement of this issue. Korea was not a signatory to the San Francisco Peace Treaty of 1951.[1] Furthermore, following the Japanese surrender in 1945 and the San Francisco Treaty of Peace of 1951, anti-Japan sentiment continued in Korea under Korea's first President Syngmun Rhee, an early leader of the Korean independence movement. In 1965, four years after Korean Army General Park Chung-hee seized power from the civilian leadership, Japan and Korea established formal diplomatic relations through the Treaty on Basic Relations between Japan and the Republic of Korea.[2] (Park himself had previously been an officer of Japan's Manchukuo Imperial Army.) These deliberations provided the South Korean government with a forum to address wartime compensation and colonial reparations. Although critics may argue that the 1965 Treaty was between "military men at the helm of repressive regimes"[3] and should not bar claims by the comfort women, Japan has long held that all WWII-related claims by Korea against Japan were settled through a separate accord (the 1965 Economic Settlement signed at that same time on property claims and protocols.

---

[1] *Treaty of Peace with Japan (with Two Declarations)*, San Francisco, September 8, 1951, *United Nations Treaty Series,* vol. 136, no. 1832, https://treaties.un.org/doc/Publication/UNTS/Volume%20136/volume-136-I-1832-English.pdf.

[2] *Treaty on Basic Relations between Japan and the Republic of Korea*, Tokyo, June 22, 1965, *United Nations Treaty Series,* vol. 583, no. 8471, https://treaties.un.org/doc/Publication/UNTS/Volume%20583/volume-583-I-8471-English.pdf.

[3] Hicks, *The Comfort Women*, 172.

Japan agreed at the time to provide Korea with the equivalent of $300 million in goods and services plus $200 million in low interest, long-term loans based on the understanding outlined in the document that "the Contracting Parties confirm that [the] problem concerning property rights and interests of the two Contracting Parties and their nationals (including juridical persons) and concerning claims between the Contracting Parties and their nationals, including those provided for in Article IV, paragraph *(a)* of the Treaty of Peace with Japan signed at the city of San Francisco on September 8, 1951, is settled *completely and finally* (emphasis added).[4] Japan thus maintains that state liability for WWII misconduct involving Korea was settled by the bilateral treaty of 1965.

Seiji Yoshida, the Bearer of False Testimony

Seiji Yoshida, a Japanese national with Japanese Communist Party ties, gained attention both in Japan and Korea by bringing the comfort women issue to the forefront in the late 1970s through his inculpatory and inflammatory text *Korean Comfort Women and Japanese People* (1977), which was followed up in 1983 by *My War Crimes—The Forced Transport of Koreans.* Yoshida "confessed" to helping to round up some 212 Korean women who were then dispatched from Korea's Cheju Island to China's Hainan Island to serve as comfort women under the guise of joining the Japanese Volunteer Corps.[5] Yoshida's work was translated into Korean and he was a key witness in confirming Japan's official role in deceptively recruiting Korean women and girls into the comfort women system.

Koreans who were in Cheju during the period that Yoshida describes in his writing denied Yoshida's allegations, and he was eventually exposed as a fraud.[6] After spending years as a "media magnet" which earned him invitations to Korea and speaking engagements in Japan to apologize for his "crimes," Yoshida finally admitted in 1996 that his accounts were fabricated. He, nevertheless, defended his actions by explaining that "hiding the facts and mixing your own assertions into the story is something that newspapers do, too."

Many Japanese felt vindicated because of Yoshida's retraction. *Asahi Shimbun*, a respected and popular left-leaning Japanese daily that had served as a mouthpiece for Yoshida's assertions, was forced to recognize its

---

[4] *Agreement on the Settlement of Problems, United Nations Treaty Series.*
[5] Julian Ryali, "Seiji Yoshida's Lies about 'Comfort Women' Exploited by Japan's Right," *South China Morning Post*, October 12, 2014, http://www.scmp.com/news/asia/article/1614619/seiji-yoshidas-lies-about-comfort-women-exploited-japans-right.
[6] Soh, *The Comfort Women*, 152–154.

role in propagating Yoshida's lies and in exacerbating tensions in Korea-Japan relations. The paper allegedly timed breaking Yoshida allegations to maximize embarrassment to Japan. They published them just prior to Japanese Prime Minister Miyazawa's 1992 visit to Korea, which made that visit an awkward one.[7]

No one wishes to be misrepresented, but those who know Japanese culture understand that such a loss of face because of Yoshida's lies was especially painful and offensive to the Japanese. Certainly, the exposure of Yoshida as a fraud was a relief for most Japanese, and Japan's denialists make much of Yoshida's fall from grace to support their position that Japan did nothing wrong.

Yoshimi Yoshiaki's Pivotal Role in Confirming the Existence of the Comfort Women System

The Japanese categorically denied that any government-supported system of indentured sexual servitude ever existed within the military until January 1992, when Chuo University history professor Dr. Yoshimi Yoshiaki revealed evidence to the contrary. Through his research, Yoshiaki uncovered official Japanese and American government archives documenting the existence of a massive military comfort women system that Japanese officials had not managed to destroy during the period between Japan's surrender and the United States' occupation of Japanese territory in August 1945.[8] The evidence uncovered by Yoshiaki confirmed Japan's official, substantive role in the creation, staffing, and oversight of the comfort station system. The documents proved that the Japanese military had set forth clear guidelines on the comfort women system and had acted upon them. Key figures reported to the Ministry of War on the system's development and progress and outlined the protocols of conduct for the comfort stations. The documents uncovered by Yoshiaki confirmed the pivotal role played by the Japanese government in establishing and implementing the system as the Japanese Empire expanded in the 1930s.[9]

Professor Yoshiaki also compiled oral histories, interviewing both comfort women and former Japanese wartime officials, and again confirmed the involvement of the Japanese government, notably through its Ministry of War, in building and maintaining the comfort stations. The documentary evidence collected by Yoshiaki also confirmed that the Japanese government

---

[7] "'Asahi Shimbun' Coverage of the Comfort Women Issue through the Years," *Nippon*, May 1, 2015, http://www.nippon.com/en/features/h00074/.
[8] Hicks, *The Comfort Women*, 57.
[9] Yoshiaki, *Comfort Women*, 42–75.

understood that such stations violated international law and they took the necessary steps to conceal such violations.[10] Because of Yoshiaki's work, we know that Japan's military and police forces, with the support of the imperial government, oversaw efforts to build comfort stations and on some occasions even helped to identify and recruit the women who could populate them.[11]

The Kono Statement: Japan's First Official Admission of the Existence of the System

As a follow-up to the evidence provided by Dr. Yoshiaki and based on further government investigation, Japan's Chief Cabinet Secretary and the official spokesperson for the government of Japan, Yohei Kono, acknowledged on August 4, 1993, the active role that the government of Japan played in the implementation and oversight of the comfort women system. The Kono Statement recognized that the comfort women's involvement in the system, in many cases, had not been voluntary and that they had been conscripted "generally against their will through coaxing, coercion, etc." Secretary Kono then went further and stated:

> Undeniably, this was an act, with the involvement of the military authorities of the day that severely injured the honor and dignity of many women. The government of Japan would like to take this opportunity once again to extend its sincere apologies and remorse to all those, irrespective of place of origin, who suffered immeasurable pain and incurable physical and psychological wounds as comfort women. It is incumbent upon us, the government of Japan, to continue to consider seriously, while listening to the views of learned circles, how best we can express this sentiment. We shall face squarely the historical facts as described above instead of evading them, and take them to heart as lessons of history. We hereby reiterate our firm determination never to repeat the same mistake by forever engraving such issues in our memories through the study and teaching of history.[12]

---

[10] Yoshiaki, *Comfort Women*, 155–165.
[11] Yoshiaki, *Comfort Women*, 60–65.
[12] Ministry of Foreign Affairs of Japan, "Statement by the Chief Cabinet Secretary Yohei Kono on the Result of the Study on the Issue of 'Comfort Women,'" August 4, 1993, 2015, http://www.mofa.go.jp/policy/women/fund/state9308.html. Commonly referred to as the Kono Statement.

The Role of the Korean Council for the Women Drafted for Military Sexual Slavery by Japan

The Korean Council, as indicated in sections above, is one of the most influential actors in the comfort women issue. The Korean Council is, among other things, responsible for the demonstrations pressuring the Korean government to not accept various deals reached with Japan, hosted outside of the Japanese embassy in Seoul every Wednesday since January 8, 1992, as well as many demonstrations supporting the comfort women statues that have been erected in Korea and the United States. For an in-depth examination of the Korean Council including its founding, its past and present roles, and the impact it has had on the comfort women issue at large, see Chapter 5 "Korean Civil Society Organizations: Accomplishments and Expectations."

Asian Women's Fund: Japan's First Attempt to Reconcile with Victims

Following the Kono Statement, Japan created the Asian Women's Fund (AWF) in 1995, described as a "joint project of the 'people of Japan' and the government."[13] The fund offered a symbolic compensation to comfort women of approximately $18,000 for each confirmed victim. It recognized Japan's role in the comfort women system and it oversaw a documented compilation of the historical record of the wrongs that Japan had committed, which remains available on the AWF website through its Digital Museum.[14] Former comfort women from several countries, including the Philippines and Indonesia, as well as allegedly some 60 Koreans that had been recognized at that time, eventually accepted AWF payouts from the fund.[15]

Japan's AWF, while a private fund, received strong moral and substantial financial support from the Japanese government, especially in documenting Japan's role in the comfort women issue through its Digital Museum and in providing compensation to the surviving victims of the system. The President of the AWF for many years was Tomiichi Murayama, the Japanese Prime Minister who, on August 15, 1995, issued the first official apology to Korea for Japan's colonial rule and for its wrongful treatment of Koreans, without

---

[13] Wada Haruki, "The Comfort Women, the Asian Women's Fund and the Digital Museum," trans. Gavan McCormack, *The Asia-Pacific Journal* 6, no. 2 (February 2008): 1–5, http://www.japanfocus.org/-Wada-Haruki/2653.

[14] "Japanese Military and Comfort Women," Asian Women's Fund, http://awf.or.jp/e1/index.html.

[15] "60 out of 207 South Korean Sex Slaves Took Atonement Pay," *Japan Times*, February 27, 2014, https://www.japantimes.co.jp/news/2014/02/27/national/60-out-of-207-south-korean-sex-slaves-took-atonement-pay/#.WanQWbLyiUk

specifically mentioning the recruitment and exploitation of Korean women and girls as sex slaves during the 1930s and 1940s.[16]

Critics in Korea, especially the Korean Council for the Women Drafted for Military Sexual Slavery by Japan, strongly opposed this initiative. The Korean Council made clear that it would not settle for less than a full and official apology at the highest level of the Japanese government (from the Prime Minister, if not the Emperor), as well as government-funded direct compensation to the comfort women.[17] The Korean Council also insisted that the enslavement, abuse, and torture of comfort women by Japan constituted a "crime against humanity." As a crime against humanity, the Korean Council held that Japan's 15-year statute of limitation would not shield the perpetrators. Beyond compensation and apology, the Korean Council thus insisted on the arrest and prosecution of those surviving Japanese war figures who played major roles in the creation and implementation of the comfort women system. AWF maintains that, when Japan first introduced its plans for the AWF to the Korean government, the Korean government "initially showed a favorable stance,"[18] but subsequently reversed themselves due to the lobbying efforts of the powerful Korean Council. The AWF persisted in offering compensation to the victims until 2007 when it ceased operations. Its website recognizes that, in the case of Korea, many of its efforts had been thwarted.[19]

The Role of U.S. House Resolution 121: Bringing the Issue to the American Public

In the United States, the 110th session of the House of Representatives passed House Resolution (H. Res.) 121 on July 30, 2007. The main sponsor of the resolution was Congressman Mike Honda, who served as the representative for California's 17th District from 2001 until 2017. Although of Japanese-American heritage, Congressman Honda has been and remains outspoken in stressing the need for Japan to face and take responsibility for this disgraceful chapter of its history. H. Res. 121 was not the first such proposed bill. As early as 1997, bills addressing the wrongs of Japan's colonial past had been introduced. The earlier bills had called upon Japan to

---

[16] Sheryl Wu Dunn, "Japanese Apology for War is Welcomed and Criticized," *New York Times*, August 16, 1995, http://www.nytimes.com/1995/08/16/world/japanese-apology-for-war-is-welcomed-and-criticized.html.
[17] "Establishment of the Asian Women's Fund and the Basic Nature of its Projects," Asian Women's Fund, http://www.awf.or.jp/e2/foundation.html.
[18] "Projects by Country or Region-South Korea," Asian Women's Fund, http://awf.or.jp/e3/korea.html.
[19] "Closing of the Asian Women's Fund," Asian Women's Fund, http://www.awf.or.jp/e3/dissolution.html.

compensate Koreans forced to serve as workers and soldiers in the Japanese military. They only included the Korean comfort women issue as one of a broader series of demands regarding injustices stemming from the 1905–1945 period of Japan's occupation of Korea.

Beginning in 2000 there was an initiative to promote political discussion in the United States on the comfort women issue. These lobbying efforts by Korean-American CSOs were strongly opposed by the Japanese government, which utilized both diplomatic channels and professional lobbyists to deter the passage of bills concerning comfort women. Over a period of several years, however, political support grew, resulting in comfort women-focused resolutions being introduced in the House of Representatives in 2005 and again in 2006. These resolutions called upon the government of Japan to recognize its role in the forced mobilization of women into a system of sexual slavery. H. Res. 121, which followed the two earlier bills, passed in 2007. It called upon the government of Japan to recognize its responsibility and provide compensation to the surviving victims of the comfort women system.[20]

The 2007 H. Res. 121 attracted 165 co-sponsors and led to a non-binding "sense of Congress" resolution that won unanimous House support. The bill gained momentum in 2007 largely due to diplomatic insensitivity and to the political clumsiness of newly elected Japanese Prime Minister Shinzo Abe.

On March 2, 2007, Abe denied that the comfort women system was involuntary and he publicly stated that Japan needed to re-assess the 1993 Kono Statement:

> There was no evidence to prove there was coercion as initially suggested. That largely changes what constitutes the definition of coercion, and we have to take it from there. [21]

Korean-Americans and Korean comfort women mobilized to express their outrage towards Abe's statement and lent their total support to lobbying in

---

[20] A Resolution Expressing the Sense of the House of Representatives that the Government of Japan Should Formally Acknowledge, Apologize, and Accept Historical Responsibility in a Clear and Unequivocal Manner for its Imperial Armed Forces' Coercion of Young Women into Sexual Slavery, Known to the World as "Comfort Women", during its Colonial and Wartime Occupation of Asia and the Pacific Islands from the 1930s through the Duration of World War II, H. Res 121, 110th Cong. (2007), https://www.congress.gov/bill/110th-congress/house-resolution/121.

[21] Colin Joyce, "Japanese PM Denies Wartime 'Comfort Women' Were Forced," *The Telegraph,* March 3, 2007, http://www.telegraph.co.uk/news/worldnews/1544471/Japanese-PM-denies-wartime-comfort-women-were-forced.html.

favor of a House resolution pointing to Japan's guilt. In April 2007 Korean-Americans placed an ad in the *Washington Post* advocating for H. Res. 121's passage.[22] In response, Japan hired a lobbying firm and ran a counter-advertisement in the *Washington Post* on June 14, 2007. The Japanese ad had a distinctive "rightist" flavor and backfired politically. Although a number of Congressmen and key leaders in the Bush Administration indicated a willingness to support Japan in the past, Abe's March 2007 comments questioning the Kono Statement, as well as the rightist advertisement, eroded U.S. support.[23]

Although Abe later rescinded his statement questioning the Kono Statement, it was not possible to reverse the damage caused by it and H. Res. 121 passed unanimously. Korean supporters of the proliferation of comfort women memorials frequently and understandably use H. Res. 121 as official U.S. government recognition of the existence of a Japanese government-supported comfort women system during WWII and of Japan's continuing failure to be forthright in accepting responsibility, apologizing, and providing reparations to the victims.

The 2014 Omnibus Legislation That Ended U.S. Neutrality on the Comfort Women Controversy

Korean groups were delighted with the passage of H. Res. 121, even if it was non-binding. They also moved forward vigorously with an effort to promote memorials to the comfort women in the United States starting in 2010. On more than one occasion, those promoting the memorials have referred to H. Res. 121 as official recognition by the United States of Japan's culpability and public irresponsibility.[24] The 2007 H. Res. 121 was later attached to the 2014 United States federal budget, which was passed by both Houses and signed into law by President Barack Obama.[25]

Congressman Michael Honda skillfully engineered the addition of the 2007 H. Res. 121 non-binding resolution as an addendum to the 2014 federal budget.

---

[22] Soh, *The Comfort Women*, 68.
[23] Tsuyoshi Hasegawa and Kazuhiko Togo, *East Asia's Haunted Present: Historical Memories and the Resurgence of Nationalism* (Westport, CT: Praeger Security International, 2008), 213.
[24] Lia Zhu, "Japan Condemned for Interference with 'Comfort Women' Memorial Lawsuit," *China Daily*, March 2, 2017, http://europe.chinadaily.com.cn/world/2017-03/02/content_28404481.htm.
[25] Park Hyun, "Bill Related to Comfort Women Passed in US Congress," *Hankyoreh*, January 17, 2014, http://www.hani.co.kr/arti/english_edition/e_international/620209.html.

After this happened, Honda assured comfort women supporters that, due to this development, the resolution would be brought to the attention of the United States Department of State.[26] Just three months after President Obama signed the 2014 budget with H. Res. 121 as an addendum, the President of the United States found himself in Seoul, Korea in a press conference with Korean President Pak Geun-hye. Mr. Obama took the unprecedented step of insisting that Prime Minister Abe and Japan address the injustices that Korean women, and comfort women in general, had suffered:

> Finally, with respect to the historical tensions between South Korea and Japan, I think that any of us who look back on the history of what happened to the comfort women here in South Korea, for example, have to recognize that this was a terrible, egregious violation of human rights. Those women were violated in ways that, even in the midst of war, was shocking. And they deserve to be heard; they deserve to be respected; and there should be an accurate and clear account of what happened. I think Prime Minister Abe recognizes, and certainly the Japanese people recognize, that the past is something that has to be recognized honestly and fairly.[27]

The rallying of the Obama administration in apparent support of the Korean position on the comfort women (and the dismissal of the contrarian Japanese view) in April 2014 represented a leap forward for Korean-American CSOs in the United States. Korean lobbying efforts were certainly not hurt by the memorials to the comfort women that had been set up across the United States between 2010 and 2014.

Following President Obama's April 2014 statement calling on Japan to accept responsibility and address the comfort women issue, *Japan Daily Press* assessed the Japanese response and reaction as follows:

> The Japanese government downplayed the prediction that the comments would trigger a new outrage. Deputy Chief Cabinet Secretary Katsunobu Kato urged the public to be cautious in their opinions, as Prime Minister Abe has already expressed regret and apology for WWII victims and their plight. He added

---

[26] Hyun, "Bill Related to Comfort Women Passed in US Congress."
[27] "The President's News Conference with President Park Geun-hye of South Korea in Seoul, South Korea," The American Presidency Project, UC Santa Barbara, April 25, 2014, http://www.presidency.ucsb.edu/ws/?pid=105136.

that the remarks "should not develop into a fresh political and diplomatic issue."[28]

Less than a year later, Prime Minister Abe received an invitation to address a Joint Session of the United States Congress where he received a warm welcome. Nine months after his speech, Japan and Korea announced that they had come to a "final and irreversible" settlement of the comfort women issue, even if bickering continued. However, with the impeachment of Korean President Park Geun-hye, the Korean government has signaled strong reservations regarding the agreement.

Hiroshima and Pearl Harbor Official Commemorations in 2016

Increasingly aggressive actions by China in the South China Sea as well as the nuclear threat posed by North Korea require a united U.S.-Japan-Korea front. When President Obama held his 2014 press conference in Seoul with President Park Geun-hye where he expressed empathy for the Korean position on the comfort women,[29] he also took steps behind the scenes to bring Shinzo Abe to address a joint session of Congress. This was followed by President Obama traveling to Hiroshima to pay his respects there in May 2016. Barack Obama became the first sitting U.S. president to empathize publicly with the victims of the August 6, 1945 nuclear attack by U.S. forces on Hiroshima. Although he did not apologize, he expressed remorse:

> We stand here in the middle of this city and force ourselves to imagine the moment the bomb fell. We force ourselves to feel the dread of children confused by what they see. We listen to a silent cry. We remember all the innocents killed across the arc of that terrible war and the wars that came before and the wars that would follow. Mere words cannot give voice to such suffering. But we have a shared responsibility to look directly into the eye of history and ask what we must do differently to curb such suffering again.[30]

---

[28] Maan Pamintuan-Lamorena, "Obama Comments on 'Comfort Women' Issue in Seoul, Urges Japan & Korea to Settle History Dispute," *Japan Daily Press,* April 28, 2014, 2016, http://japandailypress.com/obama-comments-on-comfort-women-issue-in-seoul-urges-japan-korea-to-settle-history-dispute-2847864/.

[29] "Press Conference with President Obama and President Park of the Republic of Korea," Obama White House, April 25, 2014, https://obamawhitehouse.archives.gov/the-press-office/2014/04/25/press-conference-president-obama-and-president-park-republic-korea.

[30] Barack Obama, "Speech in Hiroshima, Japan" (speech, Hiroshima, Japan, May 27, 2016), *New York Times,* https://www.nytimes.com/2016/05/28/world/asia/text-of-

This was an important symbolic gesture to Prime Minister Abe and to the people of Japan. It was followed up in December 2016 on the 75th anniversary of Pearl Harbor when Japanese Prime Minister Shinzo Abe joined President Obama in Hawaii and expressed his sympathy to the victims of that attack without apologizing for Japan's actions:

> As the prime minister of Japan, I offer my sincere and everlasting condolences to the souls of those who lost their lives here, as well as to the spirits of all the brave men and women whose lives were taken by a war that commenced in this very place, and also to the souls of the countless innocent people who became victims of the war.[31]

The Status of the December 2015 Japan-Korea Settlement of the Comfort Women Issue

The chances that the December 2015 agreement would resolve the controversy were hindered by the 2017 impeachment and jailing of Korean President Park Geun-hye, who had latched her political legacy to the December 28, 2015 "final and irreversible" bilateral settlement.[32] That settlement, following on Japan's earlier payments to comfort women in Korea and elsewhere, provided an official fund amounting to 1 billion Japanese yen or $8.3 million to create a foundation in Korea that provides assistance, solace, and healing to the 38 remaining Korean survivors identified as comfort women.[33]

The settlement included Japan's official admission of responsibility for the creation of the comfort women system, as well as a public apology on behalf of Japan by Foreign Minister Kishida Fumio. Prime Minister Abe also recognized Japan's responsibility and expressed his apology on the same date during a 15-minute phone conversation with Korean President Park.

---

president-obamas-speech-in-hiroshima-japan.html?mcubz=3.

[31] Shinzo Abe, "Rest in Peace Precious Souls of the Fallen" (speech, Pearl Harbor, United States, December 27, 2016), *New York Times,* https://www.nytimes.com/2016/12/27/world/asia/shinzo-abe-text-pearl-harbor.html?mcubz=3.

[32] Ankrit Panda, "The 'Final and Irreversible' 2015 Japan-South Korea Comfort Women Deal Unravels," The Diplomat, January 9, 2017, http://thediplomat.com/2017/01/the-final-and-irreversible-2015-japan-south-korea-comfort-women-deal-unravels/.

[33] ""Footage of Korean Women Sexually Enslaved by Japanese Soldiers in WWII Revealed for the First Time," YouTube video, segment from Arirang News broadcast, posted by "Arirang News," July 5, 2017, https://www.youtube.com/watch?v=GIC481VxVlE.

Speaking publicly on behalf of Prime Minister Abe, Kishida denounced the comfort women system and the indignities that it had dealt its victims. While the December 28 statement did not attribute any responsibility to the Emperor of Japan, Kishida did acknowledge "involvement of the Japanese military authorities at that time." He added that "the government of Japan is painfully aware of responsibilities from this perspective" and specified that Prime Minister Abe wished to express "his most sincere apologies and remorse to all the women who underwent immeasurable and painful experiences and suffered incurable physical and psychological wounds as comfort women."[34]

In his response, Korean Foreign Minister Yun Byung-se officially acknowledged Japan's position that the comfort woman statue[35] that has remained in front of Japan's Seoul Embassy since December 2011 could lead to a "disturbance of the peace of the mission" and that, from Japan's viewpoint, it represented an "impairment of its dignity." The official Republic of Korea statement read by Yun made a commitment to "taking measures such as consulting with related organizations about possible ways of addressing this issue"[36] but did not specify the steps it proposed to resolve the outstanding differences.

Bilateral relations reached an impasse as the presidency of Park Geun-hye fell apart with her impeachment. On December 30, 2016, a Korean civic group received authorization to set up a comfort women statue directly outside Japan's consulate in Busan. This happened in response to Japanese Defense Minister Tomomi Inada paying a visit to the Yasukuni Shrine immediately following Prime Minister Abe's and her return from Hawaii, where they had joined President Barack Obama at a ceremony at the USS Arizona Memorial. There at Pearl Harbor, Prime Minister Abe expressed his sincere condolences to the fallen. Abe reiterated that Japan's post-WWII constitutional commitment to peace was a "solemn vow" and he declared, "we must never repeat the horrors of war again."[37] Understandably, Koreans found that the visit to Yasukuni immediately following the return from the United States sent an unsettling message.

When the South Korean Ministry of Foreign Affairs asked Busan officials to

---

[34] Ministry of Foreign Affairs of Japan, "Announcement by Foreign Ministers of Japan and the Republic of Korea at the Joint Press Occasion," December 28, 2015, http://www.mofa.go.jp/a_o/na/kr/page4e_000364.html.
[35] Yi Whan-woo, "Japan Steps up Demand for Removal of Comfort Woman Statue," *The Korea Times*, November 13, 2015, http://www.koreatimesus.com/japan-steps-up-demand-for-removal-of-comfort-woman-statue/.
[36] Ministry of Foreign Affairs of Japan, "Announcement by Foreign Ministers."
[37] Abe, "Rest in Peace, Precious Souls of the Fallen."

remove the statue, they retorted that they lacked jurisdiction because the statue had been placed there not by the government but by a citizens' group.[38] Japan reacted by recalling Yasumasa Nagamine, Japan's Ambassador to Korea, and Morimoto Yasuhiro, Japan's Consul General in Busan. The two remained in Japan until April 4, 1917. Japan's Foreign Ministry justified the timing of their return by citing the need for Japan's presence in Korea during the tumultuous period following the impeachment of Korean President Park Geun-hye.[39]

On May 11, 2017, almost one and a half years after the "settlement" and following the impeachment and incarceration of Korean President Park Geun-hye, the statue remained in place. The *Japan News* reported that, although Japanese Prime Minister Abe urged newly inaugurated Republic of Korea President Moon Jae-in to "steadily implement the 2015 bilateral agreement" on the comfort women settlement, President Moon conveyed certain reservations, explaining that because "some people in South Korea have cautious stances on the comfort women agreement, history issues need to be resolved in a wise manner for the development of both countries."[40] Moon referred to those reservations even though thirty-four of the forty-five comfort women still alive in December 2015 had agreed to accept the compensation provided by Japan.[41] President Moon did commit to continue to work with Japan in building a joint response to the threats posed by North Korea's build-up of its nuclear arsenal and missile delivery systems. He indicated that discussions regarding settlement of the comfort women issue would be addressed in a separate track of bilateral deliberations.[42]

---

[38] "Kishida Meets with Counterpart, Demands Removal of Comfort Woman Statue in Busan," *Japan Times*, February 18, 2017, http://www.japantimes.co.jp/news/2017/02/18/national/politics-diplomacy/kishida-meets-south-korean-counterpart-demands-removal-comfort-women-statues-busan/#.WY6QjiMrKb8.

[39] Osaki Tomohiro and Aoki Mizuho, "Japanese Ambassador to Return to Korea," *Japan Times,* April 3, 2017, http://www.japantimes.co.jp/news/2017/04/03/national/politics-diplomacy/recalled-comfort-women-row-japanese-ambassador-return-south-korea-tuesday/#.WYXIviMrKb8.

[40] "Abe Urges Moon to Implement Accord," *The Japan News*, May 11, 2017, https://web.archive.org/web/20170515101332/http://the-japan-news.com/news/article/0003692793.

[41] "(LEAD) 34 'Comfort Women' Express Intent to Accept Japan's Compensation," *Yonhap News*, December 23, 2016, http://english.yonhapnews.co.kr/news/2016/12/23/0200000000AEN20161223007851315.html.

[42] James Griffiths, "South Korea's New President Questions Japan 'Comfort Women' Deal," *CNN*, June 5, 2017, http://www.cnn.com/2017/05/11/asia/south-korea-japan-comfort-women/index.html.

5

Korean Civil Society Organizations: Accomplishments and Expectations

Japan's Axis ally, Nazi Germany, committed crimes against humanity in its annihilation of Jews and other minorities between 1941 and 1945. Through the Nuremberg Trials, many of the perpetrators were brought to justice. Koreans have on more than one occasion drawn parallels between the treatment of the comfort women and the Holocaust. After the Nuremberg Trials, German Chancellor Willy Brandt offered unqualified apologies and billions of dollars of aid and compensation to the victims of the Holocaust. Germany has paid more than $90 billion in compensation and reparations to Holocaust survivors and their families.[1]

Koreans seek comparable recognition of guilt and acceptance of accountability from Japan for the criminal wrongs committed against the comfort women, and they want to revisit the 1965 agreement that released Japan from addressing Korean claims that remain outstanding. On their website, the Korean-American Forum of California, one of the most influential American CSOs supporting the comfort women, displayed a photo of German Chancellor Willy Brandt on his knees before a monument built to commemorate the hundreds of thousands of Jews from the Warsaw ghetto who perished in the Holocaust.[2]

---

[1] Melissa Eddy, "For 60th Year, Germany Honors Duty to Pay Holocaust Victims," *New York Times*, November 17, 2012, http://www.nytimes.com/2012/11/18/world/europe/for-60th-year-germany-honors-duty-to-pay-holocaust-victims.html?_r=0.

[2] Michiko Gingery et al. vs. City of Glendale, 9, No. BC556600, (S.C. Cal. Sept. 18, 2014).

The Genesis and Role of the Korean Council for the Women Drafted for Military Sexual Slavery by Japan in Seeking a Solution

Conceived of and founded in 1990 by Ms. Yun Chung-Ok, a former Professor of English Literature at Ewha Women's University, the Korean Council for the Women Drafted for Military Sexual Slavery by Japan (referred to as the "Korean Council") began its activities in November 1990. Professor Yun, a contemporary in age to the generation of Korean women and girls recruited into the comfort women system, first became active in comfort women support activities in the 1980s. Her initial focus was the Japanese sex tourism in Korea that had grown since the mid-1970s. The Korean Council describes itself as becoming "vocal in the late 1980s," and its role as that of "confronting the Japanese and Korean governments, raising public awareness of this issue within the international community, and caring for the former 'comfort women.'"[3]

Professor Yun, born in 1925, taught at the Ewha Women's University. She said that she has felt a special closeness to the comfort women. Yun recounts that, in the period of the war, her parents had her stop her studies and kept her at home. They feared that she might also be abducted and forced into sexual servitude as a comfort woman.[4] In one of its early documents, the Korean Council outlined seven areas that Japan needed to address regarding the comfort women:

- Acknowledge the crime of the Korean women drafted for sexual slavery by Japan![5]
- Reveal the whole contents of the crime of military sexual slavery!
- Apologize formally about the crime of military sexual slavery!
- Erect memorial tablets for the victims of military sexual slavery!
- Pay reparations for the survivors and the bereaved families!
- Record the crime of military sexual slavery by Japan in school textbooks and to educate younger generations about the crime in its entirety!
- Punish the criminals![6]

On January 8, 1992, the Korean Council began holding demonstrations every Wednesday in front of the embassy of Japan in downtown Seoul and calling

---

[3] Hee Soon Kwon, "The Military Sexual Slavery Issue and Asian Peace" (paper presented at The First East Asian Women's Forum, October 20-22, 1994), Macalester College, https://www.macalester.edu/~tam/HIST194%20War%20Crimes/documents/comfort%20women/KoreanWomen.htm.

[4] Kwon, "The Military Sexual Slavery Issue and Asian Peace."

[5] Exclamation points appear in the original document.

[6] Kwon, "The Military Sexual Slavery Issue."

for justice for the comfort women. Those demonstrations have continued up to the present time. On December 14, 2011, the occasion of the 1000th such demonstration, they installed and dedicated a comfort women statue in a park in front of the Japanese embassy in downtown Seoul. The statue sparked a sharp reaction from Japan including a formal protest citing Article 22(2) of the Vienna Convention, which guarantees respectful treatment of any nation's diplomatic missions abroad. The article provides that a "receiving State is under a special duty to take all appropriate steps to protect the premises of the mission against any intrusion or damage and to prevent any disturbance of the peace of the mission or *impairment of its dignity*."[7] Japan argued that the comfort women memorial statue represented an "impairment of its dignity" that could cause Japan's embassy staff to feel unfairly demeaned and threatened.

Observing Japan's reaction to the statue and the storm that followed, Koreans must have understood that they had struck a nerve. Koreans grasped that the vindication that they sought for the comfort women might best be achieved through first prevailing in the court of public opinion and not just through legislation or a court order. They apparently recognized that the erection of comfort women statues and memorials both in Korea and abroad might conveniently accelerate the realization of their goals.

On March 1, 2014, in a speech marking the 95th anniversary of the birth of the Korean Independence movement, Korean President Park Geun-hye threatened the Japanese government with "isolation" if they continued to avoid accepting responsibility for the comfort women system and the suffering that its victims endured.[8] On June 23, 2014, Korea Vice-Minister of Foreign Affairs Cho Tae-yong summoned Japan's Ambassador to Korea Koro Bessho, to the Ministry of Foreign Affairs in Seoul to protest Japan's plan to possibly revise the Kono Statement. Mr. Cho told Mr. Bessho that the international community recognized Japan's responsibility for the sexual enslavement of the comfort women and that if Japan continued to seek ways to avoid responsibility, it would lead to further marginalization of Japan from the international community. Cho stated that "the more the Abe government attempts to undermine the Kono Statement, the more its credibility and international reputation will be damaged."[9]

---

[7] *Vienna Convention, United Nations Treaty Series*
[8] "South Korea Warns Japan over Comfort Women Review," *BBC News*, March 1, 2014, http://www.bbc.com/news/world-asia-26394850.
[9] "(2nd LD) Seoul Summons Japanese Envoy over Review of Sex Slave Apology," *Yonhap News*, June 23, 2014, http://english.yonhapnews.co.kr/national/2014/06/23/77/0301000000AEN20140623002952315F.html.

While the Korean Foreign Ministry announced plans to provide more information on their website on the comfort women and also to take other steps through the development of a white paper on the subject, the comfort women memorials in the United States and elsewhere abroad have proven to be the most effective tool in stigmatizing Japan as cruel and unrepentant toward the comfort women.[10] Indeed, one can make the argument that the proliferation of comfort women memorials in small towns and cities in the United States does foster "isolation" and also damages Japan's "credibility and international reputation" as had been threatened by Park and Cho.

Korean Council Terminologies in Korea versus the United States

As it moved from the Korean to the English-speaking world, the Korean Council chose to opt for far more aggressive language in approaching the comfort women issue. The Korean name of the organization itself is 韓國挺身隊問題對策協議會 or 한국정신대문제대책협의회, which translates into English as "The Council for Establishing Policies with Respect to Problems Related to the Korean Mentality." But rather than using this rather nebulous name, the Council adopted a novel translation of the Korean organizational name and it became the "Korean Council for Women Drafted for Sexual Slavery by Japan." In English, the Council is insistent on the use of the term "sex slave," while, in the Korean literature, it uses the term "慰安婦" or 위안부 ("wianbu" in Korean or "ianfu" in Japanese), meaning "comfort or consoling woman." C. Sarah Soh has taken a critical stance toward the advocacy focus of the Korean Council, finding the organization's approach to be inadequate. Soh's writing conveys her empathy for the victims of Japan's comfort station system and her disgust for what they endured. In her book *The Comfort Women: Sexual Violence and Postcolonial Memory in Korea and Japan*, Soh shares the testimonies of several of the system's tragic victims. However, she also raises issues relevant to the positions taken by the Korean Council. Soh refers to the attitudinal underpinnings towards women within Japanese and Korean culture and argues that these views facilitated the system's emergence and acceptance at the time by the larger society.[11]

The Role of the Korean Council in Ending the Asian Women's Fund

The Korean Council played the key role in blocking the "atonement project"[12] of the Asian Women's Fund (AWF) in Korea. The fund was an attempt by the Japanese government, in conjunction with private citizens, to offer reparations

---

[10] "(2nd LD) Seoul Summons Japanese Envoy over Review of Sex Slave Apology."
[11] Soh, *The Comfort Women*, 40–41, 92–106, 197–207.
[12] "Atonement Project of the Asian Women's Fund," Asian Women's Fund, http://awf.or.jp/e3/index.html.

to the surviving comfort women beginning in 1995. In addition to offering compensation, the AWF website also told the story of the comfort women and pointed to Japan's culpability in the creation and implementation of the system. The Korean Council viewed the AWF as an attempt by Japan to avoid taking direct governmental responsibility for this criminal activity. The Korean Council also opposed this initiative by Japan because the funds, while including a direct government contribution, also consisted of donations from private individuals, thus making it less than an official act of reparation.

To persuade comfort women to spurn Japan's offer, the Korean Council lobbied the government of Korea to provide a surrogate payment to the comfort women in lieu of the proposed AWF payment. At the Korean Council's urging, the Korean government agreed to provide surviving comfort women with a modest monthly stipend to supplement the meager income that these women had available to them. The Korean Council, widely seen as the spokesperson for the surviving comfort women, called upon Japan to admit "legal responsibility for the crimes of sexual slavery" and to take steps to prosecute and punish those responsible for such crimes.[13]

The Korean Council has played an important role in the creation of the House of Sharing, a living complex created for surviving comfort women to spend the final chapter of their lives and share their stories with the many who visit the house both from within Korea and from abroad. The Korean Council has also gathered testimonies of the women who were enlisted in the system and made those available as a publication.[14] The Korean Council was led by educated women, many of whom were associated with Ehwa Women's University, one of Korea's most prestigious institutions of higher education. Their social status and the academic prestige of the Council's leadership required Korea's politicians to pay attention to them.

The Korean Council's Response to the December 28, 2015 Agreement

Almost immediately following the announcement, the powerful Korean Council rejected the deal as "shocking." *The New York Times* reported that

---

[13] "Written Submission by the Korean Council for the Women Drafted for Military Sexual Slavery by Japan" (written submission, United Nations, Committee on the Elimination of Discrimination against Women, Japan, 15 February – 04 March 2016), http://tbinternet.ohchr.org/Treaties/CEDAW/Shared%20Documents/JPN/INT_CEDAW_NGO_JPN_22816_E.docx.

[14] Keith Howard and Young Joo Lee, *True Stories of the Comfort Women: Testimonies Compiled by the Korean Council for the Women Drafted for Military Sexual Slavery by Japan and the Research Association on the Women Drafted for Military Sexual Slavery by Japan* (London: Cassell, 1995).

Lee Yong-soo, a surviving comfort woman, criticized it for falling "far short of the women's longstanding demands that Japan admit legal responsibility and offer formal reparations," and announced her intention to "ignore it completely." In the United States, the Korean-American Civic Engagement (KACE), which played a pivotal role in informing the American public about the comfort women issue and has advocated for the building of memorials in the United States, expressed "grave concerns" about the deal and expressed its resolve to continue to "educate future generations about the comfort women issue."[15]

The Korean-American Forum of California (KAFC) labeled the agreement a "sham." The Forum argued that, through the agreement, the parties were "erasing the history, as if to make it something that never happened." The Forum also expressed concern that removing the statue in Seoul would lead to removing the statue in Glendale, California, which is a replica of the Seoul statue.[16]

Representative Mike Honda described the deal as a "historic milestone" and a "step in the right direction," yet he expressed disappointment that it does not include "a formal and official apology issued by the Japanese Diet" and accused Japan of "attempting to whitewash its historic past."[17] Japan's leaders also faced strong internal opposition for failing to secure a commitment for removal of the statue in Seoul, although a government source reported that removal of the Seoul statue was an implied precondition set by the Abe administration for funding.[18] Prime Minister Abe's wife paid a visit to the controversial Yasukuni Shrine one day after the signing of the accord.[19]

On Korea's side, there are still deep reservations about the agreement.

---

[15] Jonathan Soble and Choi Sang-Hun, "South Korean and Japanese Leaders Feel Backlash over Comfort Women Deal," *New York Times*, December 29, 2015, https://www.nytimes.com/2015/12/30/world/asia/south-korea-japan-comfort-women.html.

[16] "LA Group Representing Korea's WWII Sex Slaves Denounces 'Comfort Women' Deal," Take Two, Southern California Public Radio, December 28, 2015, http://www.scpr.org/programs/take-two/2015/12/28/45724/group-representing-former-sex-slaves-denounces-dea/.

[17] Chang Jae-soon, "U.S. Congressman Honda Says Korea-Japan Deal on Comfort Women 'Historic Milestone,' " *Yonhap News*, December 30, 2015, http://english.yonhapnews.co.kr/news/2015/12/30/0200000000AEN20151230000200315.html.

[18] "'Comfort Women' Funds Won't Be Paid until Sex Slave Statue outside Japanese Embassy Removed: Source," *Japan Times*, December 31, 2015, http://www.japantimes.co.jp/news/2015/12/31/national/politics-diplomacy/comfort-women-funds-wont-be-paid-until-sex-slave-statue-by-japanese-embassy-removed-source/.

[19] "'Comfort Women' Funds Won't Be Paid until Sex Slave Statue outside Japanese Embassy Removed: Source."

Professor Kim Tae Hyun, the director of the new Reconciliation and Healing Foundation which was created through the December 2015 settlement to provide support to the surviving comfort women, was attacked and sprayed in the face with red pepper spray by a young man immediately following the opening ceremony of the Foundation on July 28, 2016.[20] On the positive side, on June 18, for the first time, it was reported that one of the surviving Korean comfort women indicated that she would accept compensation from Japan and consider this chapter closed. Those involved in negotiations with Korean civil society groups, and with the Korean Council in particular, viewed this development positively and expressed their view that if two-thirds of the comfort women were to accept, it would then become possible to negotiate with the Korean Council as well and close this chapter of history.[21]

Based on initial responses to the December 28th accord, which both countries worked to complete before the end of 2015 due in part to its historical significance as the 50th anniversary of the signing of the original Japan-Korea peace accords, the agreement represents a step forward; however, in hindsight, it is clear that it failed to heal the divide. Korean civil society groups' discontent, along with President Park Geun-hye's impeachment, led to a political reversal regarding the agreement, just as civil society groups' efforts led previously to the downfall of the Asian Women's Fund.

The United States remains pivotal in the heated exchanges that affect Korea, Japan, and East Asian security. On March 31, 2016, President Obama hosted a Nuclear Security Summit with Prime Minister Shinzo Abe and Korean President Park Geun-hye. The three leaders recognized the grave importance of collaboration among the three nations, which, as President Obama pointed out, share a "strong commitment to a rules-based order, one in which all countries, regardless of size, act according to shared norms and shared principles."[22] Due to the issue's divisive impact, before taking sides, leaders need to ascertain that they have sufficient background on this important issue or they should refrain from taking a public position.

On May 11, 2017, almost one year and half after the "settlement" and following the humiliating December 2016 impeachment of Korean President

---

[20] Sarah Kim, "'Comfort Women' Foundation Chief Is Attacked," *Korea JoongAng Daily*, July 29, 2016, http://mengnews.joins.com/view.aspx?aId=3021881.

[21] "Ex-Comfort Woman Becomes First to Back Japan-S.Korea Accord but Winning Support Not Easy," *Mainichi Shimbun,* June 18, 2016, http://mainichi.jp/english/articles/20160618/p2a/00m/0na/023000c.

[22] "Remarks by President Obama, President Park Geun-hye of the Republic of Korea, and Prime Minister Shinzo Abe of Japan after Trilateral Meeting," Obama White House, March 31, 2016, https://obamawhitehouse.archives.gov/the-press-office/2016/03/31/remarks-president-obama-president-park-geun-hye-republic-korea-and-prime.

Park Geun-hye, *The Japan News* reported that Japanese Prime Minister Shinzo Abe urged newly inaugurated Republic of Korea President Moon Jae-in to "steadily implement the 2015 bilateral agreement" on the comfort women settlement. But President Moon respectfully expressed reservations, explaining that because "some people in South Korea have cautious stances on the comfort women agreement, history issues need to be resolved in a wise manner for the development of both countries."[23] He referred to those reservations even though 34 of the 45 surviving comfort women had already agreed to accept compensation from the December 2015 settlement fund provided by Japan.[24]

President Moon's comments reflect the strong dissatisfaction expressed both by some of the surviving comfort women and by CSOs such as the Korean Council. The Korean Council maintains that the process to reach the December 2015 bilateral agreement had failed to provide an opportunity for input from the comfort women themselves and that the actions taken by the Park Geun-hye government had actually "pushed the victims into deeper despair." They also pointed out that the agreement contradicted the guidelines for resolving the problem that had been set forth by the United Nations Committee on the Elimination of Discrimination against Women (CEDAW).[25] Moon has, nevertheless, promised to continue to work with Japan in building a joint response to the threats posed by North Korea's build-up of its nuclear arsenal and missile delivery systems. He indicated that discussions regarding settlement of the comfort women issue would be addressed in a separate track of bilateral deliberations.[26]

The leading role played by Korean CSOs in driving the agenda of the comfort women cause was further punctuated by the December 2016 dedication of yet another comfort women memorial in Korea, this time directly in front of the Consulate General of Japan in Busan, the largest Japanese government complex outside of Seoul. This defiant act led Japan to recall temporarily both its Ambassador to Korea as well as the Busan Consulate General. On February 14, 2017, when the South Korean Ministry of Foreign Affairs requested that the district of Busan remove the statue; the district claimed not to have jurisdiction because it had been placed there not by the government but by a citizens' group.[27]

---

[23] "Abe Urges Moon to Implement Accord," *The Japan News*.
[24] "(LEAD) 34 'Comfort Women,'" *Yonhap News*.
[25] "Written Submission" (United Nations, Committee on the Elimination of Discrimination against Women).
[26] Griffiths, "South Korea's New President Questions Japan."
[27] "'Comfort Woman' Statue Installed near Japanese Consulate in Busan," *Japan Times*, December 30, 2016, http://www.japantimes.co.jp/news/2016/12/30/national/

Silence on American GI Sexual Improprieties: A Deliberate Blind Eye or an Unplayed Chess Piece?

While the Korean Council and its founder Yun Chŏng Ok associated Japanese sex tourism in Korea with the earlier suffering of women under the comfort station system,[28] the Council has not been vocal about the prostitution camp towns presently surrounding U.S. military bases in Korea. Those supporting the erection of comfort women statues in the United States likewise do not address this issue.

The women who served as prostitutes for the U.S. military in these camp towns were originally heralded by the government of Korean President Park Chung-hee as "Western Princesses" because, in their work as sex workers, they brought needed foreign currency reserves to Korea's national treasury. One might justifiably ask, in light of this oversight, whether the main intention of the Korean Council's activities was to support the comfort women or whether it was meant to support the Korean government and, in the process, demean and embarrass Japan.

The Korean Council has demanded that the government of Japan block all attempts to question the Korean Council's version of the plight of the comfort women. They hold that speech that dismisses the testimonies of the comfort women serves "to re-traumatize the victims through such repeated denials."[29] The Council has also insisted that future generations of Japanese be educated about this shameful chapter of Japan's history in school textbooks to assure that such a tragic injustice not repeat itself in the future.

Korea's leadership has learned both to listen to, and to recognize the importance of, civil society in continuing to "push the envelope" for justice for the comfort women. Both the Korean government and Korean and Korean-American CSOs played an important role in H. Res. 121 gaining wide support in 2007. The Korean-American community has conducted extensive outreach efforts to American political leaders apprising them of their narrative of the comfort women. These efforts help to explain why H. Res. 121 eventually gained wide acceptance.

---

comfort-woman-statue-installed-near-japanese-consulate-busan/#.WUhxQCMrLow.
[28] Lee Na-Young, "The Korean Women's Movement of Japanese Military 'Comfort Women': Navigating between Nationalism and Feminism," *The Review of Korean Studies* 17, no. 1 (June 2014): 71–92.
[29] "Written Submission" (United Nations, Committee on the Elimination of Discrimination against Women).

The Role of Korean-American CSOs in the Comfort Women Issue in the United States

Since 2010 memorials have been erected to the comfort women in locations across the United States, including New York, New Jersey, Texas, Michigan, California, Georgia, and Virginia. Brookhaven, Georgia, an Atlanta suburb, dedicated a comfort women statue in May 2017. That statue originally was supposed to have been located at the Center for Civil and Human Rights in downtown Atlanta; however, the Center withdrew its support, most likely because of complaints by Japanese groups.[30] The back and forth between Korean and Japanese groups has happened repeatedly with each new effort to establish a memorial.

Local governments have been the main supporters of comfort women monuments. Funding has originated primarily from the Korean-American community in the United States.[31] For its part, the Japanese government has worked to attempt to stop or slow the proliferation of memorials in many venues in the United States, charging that they misrepresent history.[32] Nevertheless, many Japanese-Americans, including former U.S. Congressman Michael Honda, do not concur. Congressman Honda spearheaded the 2007 U.S. House of Representatives Resolution 121, calling upon the Japanese government to apologize for sexual slavery during WWII.[33]

The Benefit Derived from Korean-American CSO Involvement in the Comfort Women Issue

When Chang Joon "Jay" Kim was elected to the U.S. House of Representatives in 1992, he became the first Korean-American to serve in the United States Congress.[34] Korean-Americans did not make further inroads at the federal legislative level until November 2018. Nonetheless, the favorable response by a number of local American politicians to the plight of Korea's

---

[30] Dyana Bagby, "Brookhaven Makes History to Memorialize Comfort Women," *Reporter Newspapers*, May 23, 2017, http://www.reporternewspapers.net/2017/05/23/brookhaven-makes-history-memorialize-wwii-comfort-women/.

[31] «Ex-Comfort Woman,» *Mainichi Shimbun*.

[32] Antonio Olivo, "Memorial to WWII Comfort Women Dedicated in Fairfax County amidst Protests," *The Washington Post*, May 30, 2014, https://www.washingtonpost.com/local/memorial-to-wwii-comfort-women-dedicated-in-fairfax-county/2014/05/30/730a1248-e684-11e3-a86b-362fd5443d19_story.html?utm_term=.ef25da93c9e0.

[33] A Resolution Expressing the Sense of the House of Representatives, H. Res 121, 110th Cong. (2007).

[34] Kim was then indicted and convicted for the solicitation and use of illegal campaign funds in his 1992 election.

comfort women has not only made the comfort women issue a hot topic, but has also helped to tell Korea's story and increase the profile of Korean-Americans, allowing them to establish important alliances. The Korean American Civic Engagement (KACE), a prominent CSO that has supported the comfort women memorials, is committed to boosting political clout for Korean-Americans in the United States. In its charter, KACE expresses admiration for the successful garnering of political influence that Americans of other ethnic origins, notably Jewish-Americans, have achieved in the United States. KACE teaches its supporters that there are important lessons to be learned from the Jewish-American community[35] and, in the cases of Fairfax, Palisades Park, and Glendale, supporters of the comfort women cause have pointed to parallels between the treatment of comfort women under Japan and the treatment of Jews during the Holocaust.

Beyond the vindication of the comfort women, Korean-Americans have other salient issues for which they seek federal support, including care for Korean-American seniors, opposition to efforts to decrease the annual number of work visas issued to Koreans, and interest in preserving the United States' commitment to protecting the Republic of Korea from an attack by Pyongyang. They have also called for the removal of references to the "Sea of Japan," the body of water located between the West Coast of Japan and the East Coast of Korea, in American textbooks. They want to replace "Sea of Japan" with "East Sea," a change which has already been affirmed by the state legislature of Virginia and been signed into law by Virginia Governor Terry McAuliffe.[36] Nevertheless, resolution of the comfort women issue remains the principal interest of the Korean-American community.

The Korean-American Forum of California (KAFC)

While various Korean-American CSOs have promoted the comfort women memorials, no American organization has gained more prominence than the Korean-American Forum of California (KAFC). KAFC has drawn a parallel between the plight of the comfort women and the Holocaust[37] and seeks comparable self-effacement from Japan, as was shown by post-WWII Germany. The December 28, 2015 agreement between Japan and Korea did not provide this, and KAFC strongly condemned the settlement, warning that

---

[35] Dongsuk Kim, "A Message to Korean-American Candidates," Korean American Civic Empowerment, December 10, 2014, http://us.kace.org/2014/a-message-to-korean-american-candidates-dongsuk-kim/.

[36] Gary Robertson, "Addition of Korean Name for Sea of Japan Becomes Law in Virginia," *Reuters*, April 3, 2014, http://www.reuters.com/article/2014/04/04/us-korea-japan-virginia-idUSBREA3301620140404.

[37] Eddy, "Germany Honors Duty."

the removal of the comfort woman statue in Seoul could lead to the removal of the statue in Glendale as well. Sylvia Yu Friedman, researcher and author of *Silenced No More: Voices of Comfort Women* (2015), characterized the December 28 agreement as "just the beginning," and pointedly observed that comfort women survivors want an apology like "the one that Willy Brandt gave at the Holocaust memorial."[38]

KAFC is headed by Ms. Phyllis Kim, who has been at the forefront of the debate surrounding the comfort women statue and memorial that were set up in the Central Park of Glendale, California. KAFC has supported efforts to establish similar memorials in other California small towns. Kim and KAFC also played a key role in the passage of legislation in July 2016 that required California schools to introduce students to the history of the comfort women in its tenth grade history curriculum.[39] With California's reputation as a trendsetter, it is expected that this addition to the curriculum will spread to other states as well.[40] Ms. Phyllis Kim has gained international attention for her efforts in making this happen, and she was invited to participate as a representative in the December 2016 opening of the Ama Museum in Taipei, which is Taiwan's first museum in honor of the comfort women.

Palisades Park: The First American Comfort Women Memorial

The first targets of Korean-American CSOs have been municipalities with significant Korean-American populations. In October 2010 the Borough of Palisades Park, under Mayor Frank M. Rotundo and then Deputy Mayor Jason Kim, a Korean-American, dedicated a stone monument to the comfort women on the grounds of the Palisades Park public library. This was the first comfort women memorial in the United States. Palisades Park, located in New Jersey near the George Washington Bridge, had a population of approximately 20,000 at the time of the 2010 U.S. Census. More than half (10,115) of the residents identified as being of Korean heritage.[41] The

---

[38] Holly Yan et al., "South Korea, Japan Reach Agreement on 'Comfort Women', " *CNN,* December 28, 2015, http://www.cnn.com/2015/12/28/asia/south-korea-japan-comfort-women/index.html.

[39] California Department of Education, "Chapter 15: Grade Ten – World History, Culture and Geography: The Modern World" in *2016 History-Social Science Framework*, 2016, http://www.cde.ca.gov/ci/hs/cf/sbedrafthssfw.asp.

[40] Victoria Kim, "'Comfort Women' and a Lesson of How History Is Shaped in California Textbooks," *Los Angeles Times,* February 7, 2016, http://www.latimes.com/local/education/la-me-comfort-women-curriculum-20160207-story.html.

[41] New Jersey Department of Labor and Workforce Development, "Table DP-1. Profile of General Characteristics: 2010: Geographic Area: Palisades Park Borough," in *2010 Census of Population and Housing*, http://lwd.dol.state.nj.us/labor/lpa/census/2010/dp/dp1_ber/palisadespark1.pdf.

monument in Palisades Park cost a little more than $2,000, which was covered by the Korean American Voters Council. The Palisades Park memorial features an etching of a Korean woman cowering before a Japanese soldier and a giant sun, with an inscription reading:

> In memory of the more than 200,000 women and girls who were abducted by the armed forces of the government of Imperial Japan 1930–1945 known as 'comfort women.' They endured human rights violations that no peoples should leave unrecognized. Let us never forget the horrors of crimes against humanity.[42]

The Payoff for Installing a Comfort Women Memorial

In conjunction with foundations and municipalities in Korea, Korean-American CSOs have invited some American officials to visit Korea. In October 2012, for instance, Palisades Park, New Jersey Mayor James Rotundo spent five days in Korea. His travel and four days of hotel expenses were paid for by the Asian Institute for Policy Studies, a non-partisan independent think tank, and the Ministry of Foreign Affairs and Trade in South Korea. While in Korea he visited the House of Sharing near Seoul, home to surviving comfort women.[43]

While there, he called for an apology by Japan at the highest level, pointing to Japan's direct responsibility for what happened.[44] Following the 2013 dedication of a memorial in nearby Hackensack, New Jersey, it was reported that Bergen County Executive Kathy Donovan, like Mayor Rotundo, had also been invited to visit Korea, and she also met with comfort women there.[45] Donovan's airfare and hotel were covered by the Korean city of Dangjin, a sister city of Bergen County.[46]

---

[42] Semple, "Memorial for Comfort Women."
[43] Alvarado Monsy, "Palisades Park Officials Detail Week-Long Trip to South Korea," *North Jersey*, http://www.northjersey.com/news/palisades-park-officials-detail-weeklong-trip-to-south-korea-1.406589.
[44] "U.S. Mayor Vows Continued Support for Wartime Sex Slavery Victims," *Yonhap News*, October 10, 2012, http://english.yonhapnews.co.kr/national/2012/10/10/0/0301000000AEN20121010010000315F.HTML.
[45] S.P. Sullivan, "Bergen County Marks International Women's Day with Korean 'Comfort Women' Memorial," NJ True Jersey, March 8, 2013, http://www.nj.com/bergen/index.ssf/2013/03/bergen_county_marks_international_womens_day_with_korean_comfort_women_memorial.html.
[46] J. Ensslin, "Bergen Executive Kathleen Donovan Headed to Korea for 6-Day Tour to Promote Business," *North Jersey*, www.northjersey.com/Bergen-Executive-Kathleen-Donovan-headed-to-Korea-for-6-Day-Tour-to-promote-business-1.453787.

A Comfort Women Statue Rebuffed in the Nation's Capital

In December 2016, there was a dedication ceremony for a comfort women statue on the capitol grounds in Washington, DC. While supporters were permitted to proceed with the unveiling on the Capitol Mall on December 10, 2016, they were obliged to remove it the following day and continue to seek an appropriate permanent location for the monument.[47] On May 14, 2014, nearby Fairfax County, Virginia inaugurated a monument near its 9/11 memorial. The dedication reads as follows:

> In honor of the women and girls whose basic rights and dignities were taken from them as victims of human trafficking during WWII. Over 200,000 women and girls from Korea, China, Taiwan, the Philippines, Indonesia, Malaysia, Vietnam, the Netherlands and East Timor were forced into sexual slavery and euphemistically called 'Comfort Women' by Imperial Japanese forces during WWII. We honor their pain and suffering and mourn the loss of their fundamental human rights. May these 'Comfort Women' find eternal peace and justice for the crimes committed against them. May the memories of these women and girls serve as a reminder of the importance of protecting the rights of women and an affirmation of basic human rights.[48]

In explaining the Fairfax County memorial, Grace Han Wolf, who is of Korean descent and a member of the Herndon City Council, as well as a key player in gaining support for the memorial, described Japan's treatment of the comfort women as "a war-crime that happened a long time ago that not many people know about, yet it happened, much like the Holocaust happened."[49] She downplayed the memorial having an anti-Japan focus. Wolf maintained that its intent was to raise awareness of the larger issue of human trafficking and explained, "We don't really perceive ourselves as anti-Japanese nor particularly pro-Korean. We were really careful to position it (the monument) that way because we didn't want it to become just about that," Wolf said. "The 'Comfort Women' is one of many sad stories about human trafficking, which

---

[47] "'Comfort Women' Statue Unveiled at Washington Event, but Permanent Site Undecided," *Japan Times*, December 11, 2016, https://web.archive.org/web/20170829095424/https://www.japantimes.co.jp/news/2016/12/11/national/comfort-women-statue-unveiled-washington-event-permanent-site-undecided/#.Wp2f6WrwaUk.

[48] Ruth Kim, "Peace Garden Seeks to Raise Awareness," *Kore Asia Media*, July 2014, http://kore.am/peace-garden-seeks-to-raise-awareness/.

[49] Olivo, "Memorial to WWII Comfort Women."

disproportionately affects Asian women and children. So we really took a pan-Asian approach."[50]

The Korean Council's Unchanging Demands

The Council condemned the December 2015 settlement almost immediately after the agreement was signed. In June 2014 at the 12th Asian Solidarity Conference on the Issue of Military Sexual Slavery by Japan, the Council reaffirmed that in order to resolve injustices and wrongdoings that the victims of the Japanese military comfort women system endured, the Japanese government should accept and recognize the following facts and responsibilities:

- That the Japanese government and Military proposed, established, managed and controlled military facilities known as "comfort stations."
- That the women were forced to become "comfort women / sexual slaves" against their will, and were kept in coercive circumstances in the "comfort stations" . . .
- That there were various forms of victimization of women from the colonies, occupied areas and Japan who suffered sexual violence by the Japanese military, that the scale of victimization was extensive, and that the suffering continues today.
- That it was a serious violation of human rights, which contravened a variety of both domestic Japanese as well as international laws of the time.

The Council has further called upon the government of Japan to take the following measures for reparation:

- Apologize to the individual victims in a manner that is clear, official, and cannot be overturned.
- Make compensation to victims as proof of apology.
- Accounting of the truth:

    1. Full disclosure of all documents possessed by the Japanese government;
    2. Further investigation of documents within Japan and internationally;
    3. Hearings of survivors and other related persons within Japan and internationally;

---

[50] Kim, "Peace Garden."

- Measures to prevent further occurrence:

    1. Implementation of school and social education including references in textbooks used in compulsory education;
    2. Implement commemorative activities;
    3. Prohibit statements by public figures based on incorrect historical recognition, and clearly and officially rebut similar kinds of statements . . .[51]

American School Children Are Mandated to Learn about the Comfort Women

Democrats and Republicans alike are in the hunt for Asian-American support and patronage; they represent America's new "swing vote."[52] Korean-American numbers are notably growing due to immigration. They represent a key demographic for voter registration and election outreach.[53] In venues where Korean-American support can make the difference in an election outcome, local politicians may feel they need to pay special attention to this constituency and many do. One of the best examples of this was the July 2016 announcement by the California Department of Education that they would include the study of the comfort women system in the curriculum of all California tenth graders.[54]

---

[51] See "Recommendations to the Government of Japan for the Resolution of the Japanese Military 'Comfort Women' Issue," 12th Asian Solidarity Conference on the Issue of Military Sexual Slavery by Japan, June 2, 2014, http://wam-peace.org/wp/wp-content/uploads/2014/07/20140602_EN.pdf.

[52] Bobby Calvan, "GOP and Democrats Slow to Woo Booming Asian-American Electorate," *Al Jazeera America*, November 2, 2015, http://america.aljazeera.com/articles/2015/11/2/gop-and-democrats-slow-to-woo-booming-asian-american-electorate.html.

[53] Taeku Lee, *Korean-Americans and the 2012 Presidential Elections* (Washington, D.C.: Korea Economic Institute, 2013), http://www.keia.org/publication/korean-americans-and-2012-us-presidential-elections.

[54] California Department of Education, "Chapter 15: Grade Ten."

6

Opposition to Comfort Women Memorials in the United States

Japan's Sense of Victimhood

Japan emerged as a major regional power with imperial aspirations at the beginning of the twentieth century. Between 1895 and 1905 it defeated two longstanding major world powers, China and Russia. Japan found and still finds much of its strength in its traditions and cultures, in which Shintoism has long played a pivotal role. Writing in 1915 on the relationship between the Japanese of his generation and those of the past, Shinjiro Kitasawa explained the centrality of revering the past, particularly commemorating those who had given their lives in service to the Emperor and the nation. Kitasawa described how in the late nineteenth and early twentieth centuries the Emperor visited the Shokon Shrine within Yasukini twice each year to pay his respect to Japan's war dead. Kitasawa also described the central role played, not by a fixed moral code but by "the promptings of conscience for ethical guidance." This approach to moral decision-making based on the "promptings of conscience" obviously invites outsiders to ask what determines good and evil if it boils down to conscience. How does one challenge the morality of a governmental decision in any situation if justified based on the assertion that a leader acted based on conscience? How can one ascertain whether a political or a military leader indeed acted based on conscience?

Shintoism emphasizes revering the past, which helps to explain the centrality of ancestral rites in Japanese culture. Kitasawa points out that, in Japanese, "the ancient term for government, *matsurigoto*" simply meant "matters of worship." Elaborating on this central dimension of Shintoism, he explains that "the reverential service to the dead, the gratitude of the present to the past, and the conduct of the individual in relation to the entire household are the chief duties of Shinto believers."[1]

---

[1] Shinjiro Kitasawa, "Shintoism and the Japanese Nation," *The Sewanee Review* 23,

The longstanding tradition of revering the past and the impossibility of determining whether historical actors felt that they acted from conscience rather than raw ambition provides some insight into the dilemma that Japan faces in assessing the morality of Japan's colonial rule of East and Southeast Asia. A significant voice in Japan still denies the mistreatment of comfort women and defends Japan's colonization of large swaths of Asia and points to the positives of modernization that Japan brought to the region, including Korea. They hold steadfast in their position that the WWII generation of Japanese deserve to be honored because they acted based on conscience. To such individuals, the war was an ethical decision, an effort by Japan to confront Western colonial powers who manipulated and exploited Asia for their own benefit. Actions taken to explicitly expand Japan's power or resource base could be understood as actions taken by Japan for the sake of freeing Asia from European influence and colonialism.

A 2005 *New York Times* article on the Hiroshima Peace Memorial Museum points to challenges that the Japanese face in coming to terms with viewing Japan as a perpetrator of war, and observes that many scholars in Japan feel a national "sense of victimhood prevents citizens from accepting responsibility for Japanese aggression against other countries."[2]

Ultranationalists defend Japan's alleged criminal behavior in the Pacific War based on the conduct of Western imperial powers in Asia and Africa, suggesting that any wrongdoings by Japan pale in comparison and that Western imperialism was not characterized by the same level of progress and prosperity that Japanese colonialism produced. Many Japanese believe still today that, through their colonization of not just Taiwan but also Korea, they improved inhabitants' circumstances. A recent Japanese publication makes this point by contrasting Japan's improvement of Korean living conditions with the exploitative colonial practices of the European powers.[3]

Japan's Efforts at Making Amends

Emperor Hirohito refused to visit the Yasukuni Shrine after the enshrinement of Japan's Class A War criminals in 1978. Emperor Akihito has not visited Yasukuni since becoming emperor, sending lesser members of the royal

---

no. 4 (1915): 480, http://www.jstor.org/stable/27532848.
[2] Martin Fackler, "Hiroshima and the Meaning of Victimhood," *New York Times*, August 6, 2005, http://www.nytimes.com/2005/08/06/world/asia/hiroshima-and-the-meaning-of-victimhood.html?mcubz=1.
[3] Hiroaki Sato, "Japan's Colonial Rule of Korea Was 'Moderate,'" *Japan Times*, June 29, 2015, http://www.japantimes.co.jp/opinion/2015/06/29/commentary/japan-commentary/japans-colonial-rule-of-korea-was-moderate/#.WYXi3yMrK1s.

household instead. However, some Japanese government ministers, including Prime Minister Shinzo Abe, have visited the shrine to pay their respects to Japan's war dead. The museum inside Yasukuni displays the final letters written to loved ones by many of Japan's suicide or Kamikaze pilots, affirming their determination to fight until the end to destroy the American enemy.

In 2005 a monument was created inside the Yasukuni Shrine to honor Dr. Radhabinod Pal, an Indian judge who served on the Tokyo War Crimes Tribunal. [4] Pal was the only judge on the tribunal who questioned both its legitimacy and its rulings. He voted to acquit all the Japanese defendants charged with Class A crimes against peace, though he did find Japanese defendants guilty of other crimes. Pal accused the United States of provoking the war with Japan through embargoes on scrap iron and oil, which led Japan to take military action.[5] In 2007 Japanese Prime Minister Shintaro Abe, on a state visit to India, made a point to travel to the home of Pal's surviving son, Prasanta Pal, to pay his respects. In an address to the Indian Parliament, Abe paid homage to Pal stating, "Justice Pal is highly respected even today by many Japanese for the noble spirit of courage he exhibited during the International Military Tribunal for the Far East."[6] The stated purpose of the Yasukuni Shrine is to console and reward the war dead. But the messaging of the shrine and the museum located there lends support to the view that the Greater East Asia War or Pacific War was not a war of aggression but a defensive war that was meant to help other parts of Asia become independent from Western colonial powers.[7]

Japan's sense of national pride runs deep, as does Korea's. While most Japanese know that manifest wrongs were committed by Japan during Japan's occupation of other Asian countries, they have shown great resistance to extending an official apology for the comfort women system from Japan's Prime Minister or from the Emperor. They also have great reservations about assailing their heritage through providing education about the comfort women in Japan's schools and in textbooks.

---

[4] "Precinct Map – 24. Monument of Dr. Pal," Yasukuni Shrine, http://www.yasukuni.or.jp/english/precinct/monument.html.
[5] Howard Zinn, *A People's History of the United States* (New York: Harper Perennial, 2003), 411.
[6] Norimitsu Onishi, "Decades after War Trials, Japan still Honors a Dissenting Judge," *New York Times,* August 31, 2007, http://www.nytimes.com/2007/08/31/world/asia/31memo.html?_r=0.
[7] Ayako Mie, "Yasukuni Shrine: It's Open to Interpretation," *Japan Times,* February 3, 2014, http://www.japantimes.co.jp/news/2014/02/03/reference/yasukuni-its-open-to-interpretation/.

The maintenance of both personal and national "face," or perceptions regarding respectability in front of others, is extremely important in Japan. The proliferation of comfort women statues in Korea and especially now in America strikes at the very soul of Japan. Koreans erect statues in the United States, denouncing Japan for its demeaning and cruel treatment of the comfort women. The Japanese as well as other students of history recognize that the Korean narrative diplomatically circumvents any discussion of American culpability for U.S. military use of the comfort women system after the war, which led to American GIs patronizing and thus enabling a prostitution ring on a massive scale in Japan, Korea, and the Philippines for decades. Unlike the Koreans, however, the Japanese are not involved in a campaign to proliferate memorials in small towns that denounce America for the bombing of Hiroshima or for the internment of Japanese-Americans during WWII under an executive order of President Franklin D. Roosevelt. Japan takes seriously statements or insinuations which challenge the pride and respectability of itself as well as others.

When American municipalities agree to erect monuments to the comfort women that make inaccurate allegations on the methods of procurement and on the numbers of comfort women, Japanese who oppose the monuments feel that the real intent of the monuments is not to defend human rights and women's rights. The monuments are viewed as an attack on Japanese character. The monuments, while embarrassing Japan, allow other actors in the comfort women travesty, including the Korean collaborators who helped to round up comfort women and the Americans who later used the system, to judge Japan with impunity.

Those Most Opposed to Exposing Japan's Past

A significant voice in Japan still denies the mistreatment of comfort women and points to ways in which the Japanese occupation of Korea and Taiwan furthered modernization in those countries. Japan's key actors in opposing the comfort women memorials include not only CSOs but parts of the Japanese government itself. Korean civil society support exceeds the support which Japanese and Japanese-American civil society opposition groups have garnered. A significant portion of Japanese society does not find offense in what Koreans have done to promote the comfort women issue.

The December 2015 settlement of the comfort women issue obliged Prime Minister Abe to rethink the denialist position that many Japanese had supported until then.[8] On behalf of Prime Minister Abe, Japanese Foreign

---

[8] Tessa Morris-Suzuki, "Japan's 'Comfort Women': It's Time for the Truth (in the Ordinary, Everyday Sense of the Word)," *Asia-Pacific Journal* 5, no. 3 (March 2007):

Minister Kishida Fumio expressed the following at the time of the December 2015 settlement:

> As Prime Minister of Japan, Prime Minister Abe expresses anew his most sincere apologies and remorse to all the women who underwent immeasurable and painful experiences and suffered incurable physical and psychological wounds as comfort women.[9]

The Japanese government, including the diplomatic corps and members of Japan's Parliament (Diet), nevertheless, remains active in opposing the proliferation of statues and memorials that reflect a Korean narrative that holds only Japan accountable and portrays other actors, including Korean collaborators who recruited for the comfort women system as well as Americans who used the system in the months following the war, as wholly blameless.

The Global Alliance for Historical Truth (GAHT)

The Global Alliance for Historical Truth (GAHT), headquartered in California and Tokyo, has strongly vocalized its objections to the Korean narrative on the comfort women issue. It has taken legal action against some of the cities that have erected memorials. Glendale, California has been GAHT's principal target.

GAHT has denounced the proliferation of comfort women monuments in the United States, especially since the 2013 Glendale decision to set up a memorial statue. On its website, GAHT explains its origins and purpose as follows:

> GAHT is based in Santa Monica, California, Tokyo and USA. It was officially recognized as a specified nonprofit corporation in March of 2015 in Japan. In the United States, on February 6, 2014, we received the official approval of California State as Non-profit Public Benefit Corporation (registration number 46-4768503). The main activities are educational activities that let you understand historical events based on facts through publications, lectures and broadcasts. These two organizations

---

1–10, http://apjjf.org/-Tessa-Morris-Suzuki/2373/article.html.

9 "Full Text: Japan-South Korea Statement on 'Comfort Women,'" *The Wall Street Journal*, December 28, 2015, https://blogs.wsj.com/japanrealtime/2015/12/28/full-text-japan-south-korea-statement-on-comfort-women/.

(i.e., the Japan and U.S.-based organizations) complement each other and cooperate and act to achieve the purpose.[10]

Dr. Koichi Mera, a Harvard-trained economist and Tsukuba University professor, serves as founding president of GAHT. In an August 2016 luncheon meeting with Tokyo's foreign correspondents, Mera described GAHT as having 15 core members as well as 500 others on their regular mailing list. Mera maintained, however, that GAHT receives donations for its advocacy efforts and that "more than 10,000 are supporting" GAHT activities.

Mera contends that today's standards should not be invoked to judge Japan's conduct during the "quite different world" of WWII. GAHT disputes the Korean position that the comfort women were "sex slaves." He contrasts the attitude toward prostitution in Asia and America:

> In this part of Asia, prostitution is a profession and not illegal. When women were born in a poor household, one way of making a living was going to that profession.[11]

The Glendale Litigation

The first full American replica of Seoul's comfort women statue was dedicated in Glendale, California, on July 30, 2013, with the near-unanimous approval of the City Council. Glendale Mayor Dave Weaver cast the only dissenting vote. Weaver deplored the "deep divide" that he believed the memorial created between Glendale and its sister city of Higashiosaka.[12] On October 1, 2013, Weaver wrote a letter of regret for the Council's vote to Yoshikazu Noda, the Mayor of Higashiosaka stating that he objected to the installation in the absence of a master plan for Glendale's Central Park, and added that he believed that the issue "is an international one between Japan and South Korea and the City of Glendale should not be involved on either side."[13] As in the case of Palisades Park, the dedication of the statue led to an official protest and a visit to Glendale by members of the Japanese Diet.[14]

---

[10] "The Global Alliance for Historical Truth," Global Alliance for Historical Truth, https://gahtjp.org/.

[11] "Koichi Mera: President of GAHT-US," Youtube video.

[12] Brittany Levine, "Mayor Dave Weaver's Letter States Regret about 'Comfort Women' Memorial," *Glendale News-Press*, November 2, 2013, http://articles.glendalenewspress.com/2013-11-02/news/tn-gnp-me-letter-20131102_1_comfort-women-japanese-imperial-army-higashiosaka.

[13] *Gingery v. City of Glendale*, 2016 Cal. App. Unpub. LEXIS 8375 (Cal. App. 2d Dist. Nov. 23, 2016).

[14] Eric Johnston, "'Comfort Women' Statues Spur Debate," *Japan Times,* February 27,

The dedication also sparked a lawsuit filed on February 20, 2014, calling for the statue's removal. Plaintiffs in the action were Michiko Gingery, a Japanese-born Glendale resident, the Global Alliance for Historical Truth-US (GAHT-US), and Koichi Mera, the GAHT-US president. These plaintiffs claimed that the monument was offensive and impeded them from using the public park. They further contended that its installation unconstitutionally intruded on the United States government's executive branch's authority to conduct foreign policy, and that Glendale's Municipal Code had not been adhered to in approving the monument.[15]

The City moved to dismiss the action for lack of standing (the actual injury required for any plaintiff to bring an action) and on other grounds, including that the complaint presented a non-justiciable political question. In opposition, the plaintiffs likened themselves to lesbian and atheist couples in the case of *Barnes-Wallace v. City of San Diego*, who were able to maintain a lawsuit against San Diego for leasing a public park to the Boy Scouts because they "[we]re offended by the Boy Scouts' exclusion, and publicly expressed disapproval, of lesbians, atheists and agnostics," contending that the leasing violated the Establishment and Equal Protection Clauses.[16]

The Glendale plaintiffs argued that they too felt excluded from a public place due to unconstitutional conduct. They claimed that in the context of international disagreement regarding the comfort women, erecting the statue in the public park violated the Supremacy Clause (U.S. Constitution Article IV, Clause 2, establishing the U.S. Constitution and federal law as the "supreme law of the land") and the separation of powers set forth in the U.S. Constitution.[17]

The plaintiffs' arguments were unavailing. In denying standing, District Judge Percy Anderson distinguished the *Barnes-Wallace* case, and ruled that the plaintiffs lacked standing to sue and failed to state a claim for relief.[18]

The Ninth Circuit Court of Appeals disagreed on the standing issue, but

---

2014, https://www.japantimes.co.jp/news/2014/02/27/national/comfort-women-statues-spur-debate/#.Wal9NCMrJo4.
[15] See Complaint for Declaratory and Injunctive Relief, *Gingery v. City of Glendale*, No. 2:14-cv-1291 (Cal. D.C, Feb. 20, 2014).
[16] *Barnes-Wallace v. City of San Diego*, 530 F.3d 776 (9th Cir. 2008) at 784.
[17] See Plaintiffs' Opposition to Motion to Dismiss, *Gingery v. City of Glendale*, No. 2:14-cv-1291-PA-(AJWx) (Cal. C.D, Apr. 28, 2014), at 14.
[18] *Gingery v. City of Glendale*, 2014 U.S. Dist. LEXIS 107598 (C.D. Cal. Aug. 4, 2014) at 11, 16.

affirmed on the issue of failure to state a claim.[19] With respect to standing, the Appeals Court noted that a plaintiff must demonstrate "(1) the existence of an injury-in-fact that is concrete and particularized, and actual or imminent; (2) the injury is fairly traceable to the challenged conduct; and (3) the injury is likely to be redressed by a favorable court decision."[20] The Court observed that Mera is a Japanese-American resident of Los Angeles who would like to use Glendale's Central Park and its Adult Recreation Center, but avoids doing so because of the monument. "[L]ike the plaintiffs in environmental cases, Mera has alleged both that he avoids public land that he would like to use again, and that his enjoyment of the park and the park's facilities has been 'diminishe[d].'"[21] The Appeals Court also found that Mera's alleged injuries were fairly traceable to the challenged conduct, and that a favorable decision would be likely to redress his injury. Thus, Mera had standing to redress Glendale's actions.

However, the Appeals Court agreed with the lower court that the plaintiffs had failed to state a claim that Glendale's installation of the Comfort Women monument is preempted under the foreign affairs doctrine. The court found that while it "is well established that the federal government holds the exclusive authority to administer foreign affairs," Glendale's installation of the monument "concerns an area of traditional state responsibility" that does not intrude on the federal government's foreign affairs power.[22]

Interestingly, in reaching that decision, the Appeals Court found it necessary to determine Glendale's "real purpose" in erecting the memorial. Plaintiffs had asserted that Glendale intended to "insert itself into foreign affairs." Relying on the language of the memorial's plaque, the Appeals Court disagreed, finding instead that

> Glendale's self-stated purposes are: (i) to preserve the "memory" of the Comfort Women, (ii) to "celebrate" Glendale's proclamation of a "Comfort Women Day" and the House of Representatives' decision to pass a resolution addressing historical responsibility for the Comfort Women, and (iii) to express "sincere hope" that "these unconscionable violations of human rights shall never recur."[23]

Given its legitimate purposes, Glendale had authority to erect the monument.

---

[19] *Gingery v. City of Glendale,* 831 F.3d 1222 (9th Cir. 2016).
[20] *Gingery v. City of Glendale,* 831 F.3d 1222 (9th Cir. 2016),1226.
[21] *Gingery v. City of Glendale,* 831 F.3d 1222 (9th Cir. 2016),1227.
[22] *Gingery v. City of Glendale,* 831 F.3d 1222 (9th Cir. 2016),1228.
[23] *Gingery v. City of Glendale,* 831 F.3d 1222 (9th Cir. 2016),1230.

Thus, the dismissal was directly based on a determination that Glendale did not seek to put pressure on Japan to come to terms with the comfort women redress movement. Nowhere in the decisions of either the District Court or the Court of Appeals is the full inscription on the monument referenced. Specifically, the Court never referenced the prefatory, and arguably most inflammatory phrase: "I was a sex slave of Japanese military."

The Appeals Court did not consider the intentions of the Korean-American civil society groups that had induced Glendale to put up the monument, and whether they sought only to preserve historical memories, or in fact wanted to exert pressure in international affairs. The United States Supreme Court declined further review of the case.[24]

A parallel California state court's litigation focused on alleged irregularities in approving the installation. The City Council was apparently not told what the text of the plaque would be, circumstances that the plaintiffs alleged were a violation of Robert's Rules of Order. In support of the plaintiffs, Masatoshi Naoki submitted a declaration to the court concerning a July 9, 2013 City Council meeting that discussed the monument. He stated that the Glendale City staff presented only a schematic diagram depicting the proposed monument. Pointedly, "[i]n response to an inquiry from City Councilman Ara Najarian as to what language would appear on the plaque," staff member Dan Bell merely stated that it would be "some general language commemorating comfort women."[25]

The court acknowledged that the City Council approved the monument without knowing what the inscription would state, but ruled that the decision to defend the lawsuit was a *de facto* approval of the inscription.[26] Perhaps the sponsors were concerned that the statement "I was a sex slave of the Japanese military" might be viewed as unacceptable in a city that is home to survivors of the U.S. WWII Japanese Internment camps.[27]

Notably, Judge Michael P. Linfield pointed to H. Res. 121 in support of his

---

[24] *Mera v. City of Glendale*, 2017 U.S. LEXIS 2032, 137 S. Ct. 1377 (March 27, 2017).
[25] *Gingery v. City of Glendale*, 2016 Cal. App. Unpub. LEXIS 8375 (Cal. App. 2d Dist. Nov. 23, 2016), at 13.
[26] *Gingery v. City of Glendale,* 831 F.3d 1222 (9th Cir. 2016), 37.
[27] See, e.g., Katherine Yamada, "Verdugo Views: Glendale Resident Recalls the Hardship of Japanese Internment Camps," *Los Angeles Times*, December 2, 2015, October 27, 2017, http://www.latimes.com/socal/glendale-news-press/opinion/tn-gnp-verdugo-views-glendale-resident-recalls-the-hardship-of-japanese-internment-camps-20151202-story.html.

ruling dismissing the lawsuit.[28]

It appears from the Glendale decisions that lawsuits to block further memorials on constitutional grounds will encounter serious obstacles. And the legal obstacles that plaintiffs would face will be compounded by public relations efforts against critics of the memorials. The Glendale plaintiffs' counsel, the Mayer Brown law firm, was subjected to withering criticism for providing legal representation to the plaintiffs. "Would any self-respecting U.S. law firm represent a client who suggested that the Jews deserved the Holocaust?" stridently asked a piece in *Forbes*,[29] although the Glendale plaintiffs had not suggested that the comfort women deserved to be mistreated. Other commentators agreed. Attorney Ken White blogged, "I cannot remember a lawsuit that so immediately repulsed and enraged. . . . This lawsuit is thoroughly contemptible. It should fail, and everyone involved should face severe social consequences."[30] Rather than continue to represent political pariahs, Mayer Brown backed out of the representation,[31] and other attorneys may think twice about the "social consequences" of objecting in court to the memorials.

GAHT and the Memorials

Notably, the Glendale memorial was viewed by GAHT as particularly offensive and led to litigation as well as official protests from the government of Japan.[32] Japanese diplomats and business representatives have also lobbied to curtail the building of monuments in New Jersey, Washington, D.C., Atlanta, Georgia, New York City, Virginia, Michigan, and in various small towns in California, as well as San Francisco.

Japan argues that the Glendale statue impedes progress in Japan-Korea deliberations. It further argues that the statue violates the U.S. Constitution, which prohibits states from building separate foreign alliances. The diplomatic

---

[28] *Gingery v. City of Glendale*, 2016 Cal. App. Unpub. LEXIS 8375 (Cal. App. 2d Dist. Nov. 23, 2016).
[29] See, e.g., Eamonn Fingleton, "'Disgusting!', Cry Legal Experts: Is This The Lowest A Top U.S. Law Firm Has Ever Stooped?," *Forbes,* April 13, 2014, http://www.forbes.com/sites/eamonnfingleton/2014/04/13/disgusting-cry-some-legal-experts-is-this-the-lowest-a-prominent-u-s-law-firm-has-ever-stooped/.
[30] Fingleton, "'Disgusting!', Cry Legal Experts: Is This The Lowest A Top U.S. Law Firm Has Ever Stooped?"
[31] Adam Poulisse, "Law Firm Pulls out of 'Comfort Women' Lawsuit against City of Glendale," *Daily News,* May 1, 2014, http://www.dailynews.com/general-news/20140501/law-firm-pulls-out-of-comfort-women-lawsuit-against-city-of-glendale.
[32] Johnston, "'Comfort Women' Statues Stir."

and legislative branches of the Japanese government began advocacy against the memorials following the 2010 dedication of the first local monument in Palisades Park, New Jersey. In May 2012 Shigeyuki Hiroki, Consul General of Japan in New York, visited the office of Palisades Park Mayor James Rotundo. According to Rotundo, Hiroki described the monument as a "stumbling block" to improving relations between the United States and Japan. [33] Rotundo maintained (and Mr. Hiroki denied) that in the course of the meeting the Consul General "offered trees, a youth exchange program between the two countries, and books for the public libraries to improve the relationship between the two countries."[34] Four members of the Japanese Diet also visited Rotundo's office on May 6, 2012. They disputed the inscription that stated that the total number of comfort women exceeded "200,000 women and girls"[35] and they also denied that these women had been "abducted." Instead they maintained that the women were fairly "paid to come and take care of the troops."[36]

As in the case of the United States, Japan's parliament (the Diet) does not speak with one voice. Those of Japan's Diet who have visited not just New Jersey but also city officials in New York, Virginia, and California represent the nationalist Liberal Democratic Party (LDP) faction within the Diet. As we have already indicated, a significant number of Japanese and Japanese-Americans, including Japanese-American CSOs, sympathize with Koreans regarding the comfort women.

For its part, the Global Alliance for Historical Truth (GAHT) denies the Korean narrative regarding the comfort women.[37] In 2013, they successfully dissuaded California's Buena Park located in Orange County where three of the five members of the City Council voted against a memorial following Japanese protests, which included a letter from the Consul General of Japan in Los Angeles. Explaining why her city had decided against the memorial, Mayor Beth Swift quipped, "we're little Buena Park!" While affirming her belief in the Korean charges of a comfort women system, she stated that this constituted an "international dispute," not an issue to be addressed by city government.[38]

---

[33] Chloe B. Park, "Japanese Effort to Remove N.J. 'Comfort Women' Monument Angers Koreans," Voices of NY, May 10, 2012, https://voicesofny.org/2012/05/japanese-effort-to-remove-nj-comfort-women-monument-angers-koreans/.
[34] Park, "Japanese Effort to Remove N.J. 'Comfort Women' Monument Angers Koreans."
[35] Park, "Japanese Effort to Remove N.J. 'Comfort Women' Monument Angers Koreans."
[36] Semple, "Memorial for Comfort Women."
[37] "Koichi Mera: President of GAHT-US," Youtube video.
[38] Brittany Levine, "Comfort Women Statue Opponents Sway Buena Park," Los

GAHT Activities in the United States

As discussed above, GAHT took the City of Glendale to court for the comfort women "Statue of Peace" that Glendale erected in the city's Central Park. In a talk that GAHT founder Koichi Mera delivered to foreign press correspondents in Tokyo in 2016, he explained that "the honor of Japanese people will be seriously damaged" if lower court rulings defending the presence of the Glendale statue are allowed to stand (they were), and he announced GAHT's intention to appeal this matter to the Supreme Court (which it did without success).[39] Mera noted that more than 30 comfort women statues have been installed throughout Korea, and claimed that there were plans for the erection of some 20 such statues in the United States. Mera believes that GAHT's willingness to litigate can serve as a deterrent to more statues, because municipalities must consider the outlay of significant funds in court cases defending their decisions.[40]

> Mera dismisses the testimonies of many of the Korean women who have come forward identifying themselves as comfort women. In his book *Comfort Women Not "Sex Slaves"* (2015), Mera relies largely on one 1944 United States Office of War Information Interrogation Report. The report, drawn up by Staff Sergeant Alex Yorichi, a Japanese-American, was based on interviews with 19 Korean women who served as comfort women in Burma. The report states that a "comfort girl" was "nothing more than a prostitute" and suggests that the women involved were "whimsical, and selfish" and lived in "near luxury." Importantly, the report does, however, confirm that the women found in Burma claim to have been recruited under false pretenses, having been promised "easy work" and "plenty of money" for completing tasks such as "visiting the wounded in hospitals, rolling bandages and generally making the soldiers happy."[41]

Defenders of Japan's conduct, such as Mera, seem to focus on the parts of the Burma interrogation that support their claims.[42] Mera does admit to the

---

Angeles Times, July 27, 2013, http://www.latimes.com/tn-gnp-me-comfort-women-statue-opponents-sway-buena-park-20130727-story.html.

[39] "Koichi Mera: President of GAHT-US," Youtube video.
[40] "Koichi Mera: President of GAHT-US," Youtube video.
[41] United States Office of War Information, "Japanese Prisoner Interrogation Report No. 49," conducted by T/3 Alex Yorichi, October 1, 1944, https://upload.wikimedia.org/wikipedia/commons/6/68/Japanese_Prisoner_of_War_Interrogation_Report_No._49_p1.png.
[42] "Koichi Mera: President of GAHT-US," Youtube video.

mistreatment of some women who were taken by the Japanese military in the Dutch East Indies and in the Philippines but does not see a similar pattern in the treatment of Taiwanese and Korean comfort women.[43] While Mera's book includes Yoshimi Yoshiaki's *Comfort Women* in its bibliography, he focuses on exposing the fallacious testimony of Seiji Yoshida, whom we have already discussed. In 1996 Yoshida admitted that his account was fictitious. While Mera points to Yoshida's misrepresentation and to the Burma testimonies, he does not comment on the more than 250 testimonies of Taiwanese and Korean women who, beginning in 1990, came forward and identified themselves as "comfort women" and shared their experiences.

Using the Burma report, Mera asserts that the comfort women earned 50 times what the Japanese soldier earned in a month. He questions how there could possibly have been 200,000 women because, if there had been, the Japanese soldiers would have had "no time to fight."[44] Mera denies Japanese government involvement in recruiting. He points instead to private agents. The military, he asserts, limited its involvement to providing accommodations as well as a weekly medical check-up and a careful monitoring of the women's working hours. Mera argues that the comfort women were citizens of Japan and thus received equal treatment to what Japanese women would receive. Mera also includes scanned copies of ads made to recruit comfort women that had been placed in Korean publications, which clearly explained what the women were going to be doing.[45]

In his August 2016 press conference in Tokyo, Mera questioned the motivation of the Korean and the Korean-American civil society groups involved in the proliferation of memorials. Mera believes that the main purpose of Korean efforts for the comfort women is to humiliate Japan.[46]

Mera is also wary of recent Chinese-American activism on the comfort women issue by the Justice Coalition in California. In particular, Mera identifies former California Judges Lillian Sing and Julie Tang who have become increasingly outspoken on the comfort women issue. Mera speculates on ties between this group and the pro-Beijing Global Alliance for Preserving the History of the Second World War in Asia, which actively promoted Iris Chang's book *The Rape of Nanking*. Mera challenges the historical accuracy of Chang's account of events and speculates that "the Rape of Nanking itself may not have taken place." He believes that a

---

[43] "Koichi Mera: President of GAHT-US," Youtube video.
[44] "Koichi Mera: President of GAHT-US," Youtube video.
[45] Koichi Mera, *Comfort Women Not 'Sex Slaves:' Rectifying the Myriad of Perspectives* (Bloomington, IN: Xlibris, 2015), 13.
[46] "Koichi Mera: President of GAHT-US," Youtube video.

relationship exists between recent Chinese and Chinese-American civil society advocacy for the comfort women and the People's Republic of China. For Mera, China's intention in supporting these efforts is to "try to break up the U.S.-Japan relationship as Chinese are doing in the case of Okinawa."[47] Mera does not support the December 2015 agreement between Japan and Korea: "I cannot control the behavior of the Japanese government. Mr. Abe has his own freedom in choosing policies." He states that the payment "looks like an admission of guilt."

When asked if he had ever tried to engage the Korean CSOs in dialogue regarding the comfort women, Mera suggests that the Koreans have indicated that they have no interest in such dialogue.[48]

While the concept of "saving face" is well known throughout Asia, there is perhaps no country more sensitive to this than Japan. Those who have regularly interfaced with the Japanese know how challenging it is for them to point out the wrongdoings of others. They only do so with great hesitation and self-effacement. The Japanese want to be offensive to no one, but implicit in this practice is also the expectation that others will not be needlessly offensive to them. This desire not to offend applies also to hostile powers who have acted against Japan. Whereas other groups who have suffered offenses at the hands of the United States or the major European powers are wont to decry the crimes of "foreign interlopers," the Japanese are reticent to do so. Displays in Hiroshima testify to the horrors of nuclear weapons, rather than indict the United States for having used them in a place with such a large civilian population.

Japanese Behaviors and Practices that Koreans Find Offensive

Certainly, one of the most disturbing issues to other countries is Japanese devotion to the Yasukuni Shrine, especially in the case of any devotion shown by members of Japan's political elite. As we have seen, immediately following the Prime Minister's and Minister of Defense's return from a December 2016 visit to Pearl Harbor, Defense Minister Tomomi Inada paid a visit to the Yasukuni Shrine.[49] This visit sparked a negative reaction from China and Korea and led to the permanent placement of a comfort women statue in front

---

[47] "Koichi Mera: President of GAHT-US," Youtube video.
[48] "Koichi Mera: President of GAHT-US," Youtube video.
[49] Elaine Kurtenbach, "Japan's Defense Minister visits Yasukuni after Pearl Harbor," *Washington Post,* December 29, 2016, https://www.washingtonpost.com/world/japans-defense-minister-visits-yasukuni-after-pearl-harbor/2016/12/29/79119c84-ce02-11e6-b8a2-8c2a61b0436f_story.html?utm_term=.01238be6ce74.

of the Japanese Consulate-General in Busan.[50]

For their part, the Japanese are increasingly frustrated with Korean efforts to continue recriminations from the last century. The Japanese expect the world to regard post-war Japan as a "new Japan," and appreciate that the Japanese Constitution states in Article 9 of Chapter 2 that "the Japanese people forever renounce war as a sovereign right of the nation and the threat or use of force as means of settling international disputes."[51] As a Japanese woman queried, "Why can't all of Japan's humanitarian efforts and our disaster relief work be seen as atoning for the past?"

---

[50] "'Comfort Woman' Statue Installed near Japanese Consulate in Busan," *Japan Times*, December 30, 2016, http://www.japantimes.co.jp/news/2016/12/30/national/comfort-woman-statue-installed-near-japanese-consulate-busan/#.WWIXwumgfzI.

[51] Kenpo (Constitution of Japan), November 3, 1946, chap. 2, art. 9, http://japan.kantei.go.jp/constitution_and_government_of_japan/constitution_e.html.

7

The Unusual Case of Taiwan

Besides Korea, Taiwan is the only country that was annexed by Japan in the period leading up to WWII. Taiwanese and Koreans shared the experience of Japanese colonial rule. When one visits Taiwan, one discovers a more positive and appreciative attitude towards Japan than one finds in Korea, which does not conceal its deep feelings of resentment. Although no doubt much less in number, Taiwanese comfort women, like their Korean counterparts, were forced to provide sexual services to Japan's military. Nevertheless, while 38 statues and monuments honor the memory of the comfort women throughout Korea, only one such statue can be found in Taiwan. Unlike Korea, Taiwan has erected monuments to pay homage to Japan, honoring the contribution that Japanese made to Taiwan during the colonial period.

Taipei opened its first comfort women museum in December 2016. The museum clearly points to Japan's culpability for the comfort women system. It further goes on to suggest practical ways that the comfort women ordeal can inform today's efforts to end human trafficking and domestic violence in Taiwan, crimes which stem from a demeaning view of women.

In May 2016 when President Tsai Ing-wen was inaugurated as Taiwan's president, members of her Democratic Progressive Party (DPP) called upon her to rethink how Taiwan remembers the Republic of China's founding president Chiang Kai-shek. A debate has surged about whether or not to demolish or repurpose the spacious park grounds, facilities, and museum in downtown Taipei that currently celebrate Chiang Kai-shek's achievements.[52] In the spring of 2017, three public statues of Chiang were vandalized and decapitated.[53]

---

[52] "Leave Chiang Kai-shek Memorial Hall Alone," *China Morning Post*, May 6, 2016, https://web.archive.org/web/20160511181648/http://www.chinapost.com.tw/editorial/taiwan-issues/2016/05/06/465247/leave-chiang.htm.

[53] Hideshi Nishimoto, "Chiang Kai-shek Statue Beheaded in Taiwan in Latest Incident," *Asahi Shimbun*, April 23, 2017, http://www.asahi.com/ajw/articles/

While Chiang is viewed critically, some of the Japanese who lived in Taiwan during the colonial period are fondly remembered. In the city of Tainan, there is an annual ceremony to celebrate the life of Japanese civil servant Yoichi Hatta. The Taiwanese participants in the ceremony offer flowers and deep bows to Hatta's statue in the park, paying homage to his role in turning "the infertile land of southern Taiwan into an abundant 'rice barn.'"[54]

The Taiwanese recognize Japan's role in the development of Taiwan's trained workforce, in the modernization of its irrigation systems, in the building of the Taiwanese railway system,[55] and in the design and creation of many of Taiwan's major government buildings.[56] The favorable recollections that most Taiwanese harbor towards the period under Japanese rule help to explain their reservations toward criticizing Japan for its callous mishandling of the comfort women issue. Any such campaign, they fear, could destabilize the greatly valued bilateral ties that Taiwan holds with Japan.

Japan's Annexation of Korea and Taiwan

In the final decade of the nineteenth century, Japan had its eyes set on becoming an imperial power like France, England, and Holland. Japan modernized its military, including its naval forces, in the years following the March 31, 1854 Convention of Kanagawa between U.S. Commodore Matthew Perry and the ruling Tokugawa shogunate. Following the first Sino-Japanese War in 1895, which took place primarily over Japan's efforts to gain control of Korea, Taiwan was ceded to Japan by China's ruling Qing Dynasty through the 1895 Treaty of Shimonoseki.

Korea sought out Russian support to avoid falling under Japanese control, leading to the Russo-Japanese War in 1904. Once again, Japan prevailed, and, following the Treaty of Portsmouth (New Hampshire), Japan felt supported by the United States in its efforts to gain control of Korea. In 1905, through the Eulsa Treaty of Protection, Korea fell largely under Japan's control and was fully annexed in 1910. Japan later recognized the inhabitants of Korea and Taiwan as subjects of Japan and granted them citizenship. Because they were subjects of Japan, Taiwanese and Korean comfort women

---

AJ201704230023.html.
[54] Chiu Yu-tzu, "Japanese Pioneer Remembered," *Taipei Times*, May 5, 2000, http://www.taipeitimes.com/News/local/archives/2000/05/05/34805.
[55] "Railway Diplomacy," *Taiwan Today*, May 1, 2015, http://taiwantoday.tw/news.php?unit=8,29,32&post=14202.
[56] "Taiwan President Says Should Remember Good Things Japan Did," *Reuters*, October 25, 2015, http://www.reuters.com/article/us-taiwan-china-idUSKCN0SJ03Y20151025.

were viewed differently than the women taken by the Japanese military in places such as the Philippines, Malaysia, Indonesia, or China. The latter groups were seen as the "spoils of war" as opposed to an auxiliary force to the Japanese military who were performing an important patriotic duty.

Taiwan's versus Korea's Experience of Japanese Colonial Rule

In spite of both Korea and Taiwan having been Japanese colonies and both having had women conscripted as comfort women, Taiwan's historical memory of the period under Japan contrasts with Korea's. Taiwan was Japan's first colony, acquired in 1895, 15 years prior to Japan's full annexation of Korea. Japan's leadership considered success in its colonization efforts in Taiwan as key in gaining recognition from the West that Japan had indeed "arrived" as an imperial power.[57] Japan wanted to demonstrate that it could not only govern as an imperial power, but that it could actually improve the living conditions of the inhabitants of its colonies.[58] Japan played a major role in modernizing Taiwan and promoted local self-rule by the Taiwanese. Japan also contributed to Korea's modernization and to local self-rule; however, the period in Taiwan after WWII under Chiang Kai-shek is seen by most Taiwanese as a second, more oppressive colonial period than the years under Japanese rule.

The Taiwan Experience under Japan

When Taiwan was ceded to Japan in 1895 through the Treaty of Shimonoseki, local Taiwanese leaders at first made an effort to establish an independent Republic of Formosa and resist annexation. Some level of local resistance to Japan's annexation of Taiwan continued for decades. The Tapani Incident of 1915 and the Wushe Uprising of 1930 stand as the most remembered acts of Taiwanese resistance to Japanese rule. In 1915, Taiwanese locals of Han Chinese origin, affiliated with a local Buddhist sect, carried out a series of "armed attacks against police stations;" the Japanese crackdown that followed resulted in the deaths of some 1,412 Taiwanese of Han Chinese origin and "another 1,424 were arrested and sentenced by the Japanese colonial government."[59] The Tapani Incident represented the final major armed revolt against Japanese rule led by Taiwanese of Han origin.

The 1930 Wushe Uprising was led by the Seediqs, one of Taiwan's aboriginal

---

[57] Leo T. S. Ching, *Becoming 'Japanese:' Colonial Taiwan and the Politics of Identity Formation* (Berkeley: University of California Press, 2001), 17.
[58] Ching, *Becoming 'Japanese:' Colonial Taiwan and the Politics of Identity Formation*.
[59] Tapani Incident Centennial Marked by Tainan City," *Taiwan Today*, June 9, 2015, https://taiwantoday.tw/news.php?unit=2&post=3673.

tribes. In October 1930 the Japanese district governor came to officiate over Wushe's annual sports competition accompanied by scores of other Japanese military and civilians. An armed contingent of "300 aboriginal men in native attire and armed with rifles, guns, and swords" attacked the Japanese delegation, killing 134 of them, including not only the Japanese police commissioner and soldiers who participated but Japanese civilians as well, including women and children. In response, the Japanese mobilized some 3,000 troops. They killed 214 Seediq warriors and their family members.[60]

The Japanese military leaders who presided over the Wushe crackdown received harsh reprimands from the government of Japan. Japan had hoped to be recognized for improving the well-being of its colonies rather than for repressing them. After the Wushe uprising, Japan adopted new policies aimed at treating Taiwan's aboriginal population with greater respect, "as imperial subjects assimilated into the Japanese national polity through the expressions of their loyalty to the emperor."[61]

Rule under Japan versus Rule under Chiang Kai-shek

Koreans understandably harbor deep, unsettled feelings of resentment due to Japan's failure to openly accept responsibility and fully apologize for their actions during the colonial period. They can point to Japan's brutal torture and execution of Korean independence leaders, to the persecution of Korean Christians who objected to emperor worship, to the suppression of the Korean language and culture, to the confiscation of Korean families' food supplies, and to the forced mobilization of Koreans as slave laborers, soldiers, and comfort women.[62] Although the Taiwanese had memories such as Tapani and Wushe, their historical memory of suffering under Japan softened due to what the island experienced after its "liberation" following WWII by the Kuomintang (KMT) forces of Generalissimo Chiang Kai-shek.

In August 1945 the island's inhabitants, including the Han Chinese whose family ties to Taiwan, which in most cases traced back centuries, celebrated the end of five decades of Japanese occupation; however, this elation soured soon after the arrival of Chiang's KMT representatives. Dispatched to accept the surrender of Japan's occupying army, they showed little patience for Taiwanese resistance. A ruthless crackdown began on February 28, 1947, an event referred to as the "February 28 Incident" or the "228 Incident." One day prior on February 27, KMT security forces apprehended and publicly

---

[60] Ching, Becoming 'Japanese,' 138-139
[61] Ching, Becoming 'Japanese,' 152.
[62] Michael Breen, The Koreans: Who They Are, What They Want, Where Their Future Lies (New York: Thomas Dunne Books, 2004), 103–115.

interrogated Ms. Lin Jiang-mai, a 40-year-old widow, for allegedly selling contraband cigarettes at her vending stand in Taipei. The KMT security forces seized both her contraband product as well as her inventory of government-sanctioned cigarettes. They also impounded the earnings from her sales. When Ms. Lin protested, she was struck on the head with a gun by KMT security forces.[63]

Her pleas for mercy attracted a sympathetic local crowd and sparked their indignation. Intimidated by the crowd's outcry, the KMT forces fled the scene but not before firing into the crowd, killing one person. This led to nationwide protests the following day, calling for the arrest and punishment of the persons responsible for the previous day's shooting. The KMT reacted callously, killing an estimated 18,000 to 28,000 Taiwanese protesters and activists over the next few weeks. The 228 Incident and its aftermath provided the KMT with a rationale for implementing the 38 years of martial law that followed, commonly referred to as the "White Terror." With the 1949 collapse of Chiang Kai-shek's Nanjing government, forcing his flight to Taipei, the KMT further tightened its grip. Furthermore, for the next two decades, Taipei would serve as the *de facto* capital of what the United Nations would recognize as "China" until the Beijing government assumed the UN seat on October 25, 1971.

The four-decade long period of White Terror repression under Chiang Kai-shek and then his son Chiang Qing-kuo stifled political dissent and any effort for Taiwanese independence. Violations of the stringent limitations imposed on speech and assembly by the Chiangs resulted in severe reprisals.[64] Grandparents, parents, other close relatives, as well as friends of many of today's Taiwanese endured imprisonment and torture between 1949 and 1987. The accounts of the KMT's punitive and vindictive comportment during this period help to explain why today most Taiwanese have developed an increasingly benign view of Japanese colonial rule compared to the experience under Chiang Kai-shek and his son.

In 1997 President Lee Teng-hui, the first Taiwanese native to serve as president of Taiwan, inaugurated the 228 Museum. It serves as a constant reminder that KMT rule led to tens of thousands of Taiwanese being subjected to arrests and torture including at least 1,200 summary

---

[63] Flora Wang, "The 228 Incident: Sixty Years on—Taipei Documentary Provokes Outrage," *Taipei Times*, February 28, 2007, http://www.taipeitimes.com/News/taiwan/archives/2007/02/28/2003350348.

[64] "About the February 28 Incident," 228 Memorial Museum, Taipei Government, May 4, 2015, http://228memorialmuseum.gov.taipei/ct.asp?xItem=1938462&ctNode=41711&mp=11900A.

executions.⁶⁵ Past authoritarian KMT rule, along with Beijing's persistent, strident calls for "One China" and Beijing's own repressive history help to explain the positions taken by recent independence-minded CSOs in Taiwan, including the youth-led Sunflower Movement, which in 2015 spearheaded calls for Taiwanese *de jure* independence from the mainland.⁶⁶ Mainland China, in spite of its criticism of Chiang Kai-shek, has not endeared itself to Taiwan. For some, the 1989 Tiananmen Square crackdown by Beijing revived haunting memories of the 228 incident.⁶⁷ The *Taipei Times* as well as a number of other Taiwanese publications report that the PRC detains not only human rights activists but the attorneys who dare to defend them.⁶⁸

One popular Taiwanese saying describes the change from Japanese to KMT rule in Taiwan as "the dogs (the Japanese) left but the pigs (KMT) came."⁶⁹ Taiwanese history professor Lung-chih Chang explains that "dog," which is used here to represent Japan, implies tight control and repression but that, in spite of this, the dog's "discipline" leads to order and predictability. On the other hand, the "pig," depicting KMT rule, is also characterized by force and repression; however, rule by "pigs" does not result in the same order and predictability that one finds when ruled by "dogs."⁷⁰ The accommodating recollections that most Taiwanese now harbor towards their period under Japanese rule explain why many Taiwanese prefer to downplay the need for Japan to accept responsibility, offer an official apology and compensate the few surviving Taiwanese victims. Such an approach, they fear, would destabilize bilateral ties.

A dissenting view on Japanese colonization of Taiwan, nevertheless, finds unsettling ways of expression. On April 17, 2017, Lee Cheng-lung, a former Taipei City Councilor and an activist in Taiwan's small China Unification Promotion Party, along with an accomplice, took the extraordinary step of

---

⁶⁵ Cindy Sui, "Taiwan Kuomintang: Revisiting the White Terror Years," *BBC News*, March 13, 2016, May 14, 2017, http://www.bbc.com/news/world-asia-35723603.
⁶⁶ Cindy Sui, "Will the Sunflower Movement Change Taiwan?" *BBC News*, April 9, 2015, http://www.bbc.com/news/world-asia-32157210.
⁶⁷ Li Thian-hok, "The 228 Incident and Tiananmen Square," *Taipei Times*, February 28, 2001, http://www.taipeitimes.com/News/editorials/archives/2001/02/28/0000075544.
⁶⁸ "Trial of Lawyer Accused of Subversion Starts in China," *Taipei Times*, May 9, 2017, http://www.taipeitimes.com/News/world/archives/2017/05/09/2003670246; Stephen Gregory, "Human Rights Lawyers Shine in China, but need the World to Notice," *The Epoch Times*, May 22, 2017, http://www.theepochtimes.com/n3/2251896-human-rights-lawyers-shine-in-china-but-need-the-world-to-notice/.
⁶⁹ Xiaokun Song, *Between Civic and Ethnic: The Transformation of Taiwanese Nationalist Ideologies (1895-2000)* (Brussels: VUB Press, 2009), 128.
⁷⁰ Dr. Lung-chih Chang (research fellow, Institute of Taiwan History, Academia Sinica), in discussion with the author, September 30, 2016.

decapitating the Yoichi Hatta statue in Tainan. Lee boasted of his actions on *Facebook* and turned himself in to police in Taipei. However, he refused to reveal where he had hidden the statue's missing head.[71] Tainan city officials, acting quickly, repaired the damaged statue. On May 7 Tainan Mayor William Lai, together with members of the Hatta family, participated in a rededication ceremony. Lai "apologized to the Hatta family for the city's failure to protect the statue," and, with heightened security, the restored statue was ready on schedule for the annual May 8 ceremony honoring Hatta.[72] On April 22, just five days after the Hatta incident, a statue of Chiang Kai-shek was decapitated in a park "on the outskirts of Taipei." Red paint was dumped on both the statue and the decapitated head. "228" was spray-painted on the statue base.[73]

Taiwan's Resistance to Partnership with Beijing on the Comfort Women Issue

In October 2016, China unveiled a sculpture at Shanghai Normal University commemorating Chinese comfort women.[74] Beijing has recently demonstrated a growing interest in promoting the comfort women cause and reminding the world of the crimes committed by Japan during the 1930s and 1940s. Their efforts have been reinforced by some Chinese and Chinese-Americans in the United States. [75] A state dedicated in Seoul in October 2015 portrays a Korean comfort woman and a Chinese comfort woman seated beside each other. The South Koreans who organized the ceremony told the *New York Times* that "they planned to build replicas of the same sculpture in Shanghai and San Francisco." In explaining the basis of China's bond with Koreans, Leo Shi Young, a Chinese-American filmmaker and key supporter of the project, noted that "Koreans and Chinese resisted together like brothers against Japanese aggressions."[76]

---

[71] Wang Kuan-jen and William Hetherington, "Pair Surrenders to Police over Hatta Statue Decapitation," *Taipei Times,* April 18, 2017, http://www.taipeitimes.com/News/front/archives/2017/04/18/2003668927.
[72] Wang Han-ping and William Hetherington, "Mayor Attends Hatta Statue Unveiling," *Taipei Times*, May 8, 2017, http://www.taipeitimes.com/News/taiwan/archives/2017/05/08/2003670179.
[73] Nishimoto, "Chiang Kai-shek Statue Beheaded."
[74] Peipei Qiu, *Chinese Comfort Women: Testimonies from Imperial Japan's Sex Slaves* (New York: Oxford University Press, 2013), 38.
[75] Tomo Hirai, "S.F. Board Unanimously Passes 'Comfort Women' Memorial Resolution," New America Media, October 6, 2015, http://newamericamedia.org/2015/10/sf-board-unanimously-passes-comfort-women-memorial-resolution.php.
[76] Choe Sang-Hun, "Statues Placed in South Korea Honor 'Comfort Women' Enslaved for Japan's Troops," *New York Times,* October 28, 2015, https://www.nytimes.

Too firm an alliance with Korea, because of its strong ties with mainland China on the comfort women issue, is not a prudent option for Taiwan. It could undermine long-term Taiwanese political interests in remaining separate from China. Taiwan needs lasting, positive ties with Japan. Taiwanese citizens do not wish to be seen as Chinese nationals or as outliers destined to join the PRC.

The Comfort Women Experience in Taiwan

In her interviews with Taiwanese comfort women, Dr. Chu Te-lan, a senior researcher in Academia Sinica's Research Center for the Humanities and Social Sciences and recognized authority on Taiwan's comfort women, found that only three of the women whom she interviewed understood at the time of their conscription that they would serve as sex workers.

The other comfort women interviewed by Chu stated that they had been misled by recruiters, just as most Korean comfort women had been deceived by their handlers' false promises.[77] Taiwan's victims had received assurances that they would serve as entertainers, barmaids, office workers, and nurses[78] but certainly not as sex workers. Their deceptions in recruitment mirror those of most Korean comfort women.

In spite of parallel testimonies on recruitment, the estimated number of Korean women recruited into the comfort women system greatly outnumbers Taiwanese women. Chu estimates only 1,000 women in Taiwan were conscripted,[79] whereas the Taipei Women's Rescue Foundation (TWRF) estimates at least 2,000 women.[80] Both of these figures "pale" in comparison to the tens of thousands of Korean women and girls thought to have been conscripted.[81]

Navigating between Tokyo and Beijing: Lessons from the Ama Museum

Based on the definitive evidence of Taiwanese comfort women provided by

---

com/2015/10/29/world/asia/south-korea-statues-honor-wartime-comfort-women-japan.html.

[77] Howard, *True Stories*, 32–192.
[78] Howard, *True Stories*.
[79] Dr. Chu Te-lan and Dr. Lung-chih Chang (research fellows, Research Center for Humanities and Social Sciences and Institute of Taiwan History, Academia Sinica), in discussion with the author, October 18, 2016.
[80] Lai et al., *Silent Scars*, 28.
[81] "7. How Have the Women Lived after the War?," Fight for Justice, http://fightforjustice.info/?page_id=2772&lang=en.

Ms. Itoh Hideko, followed by the first Taiwanese women coming forward and identifying themselves as former comfort women, Taiwan's Legislative Yuan established a Taiwanese Comfort Women Investigation Committee in 1992. One outcome of their deliberations was to delegate the Taipei Women's Rescue Foundation (TWRF), a local Taipei NGO, as the sole "focal point for efforts to solve the comfort women issue in Taiwan," assigning it the responsibility to: "1. identify former comfort women; 2. handle information on individuals; and 3. act as an agent in transmitting to them government subsidies for their living expenses."[82]

Through a documentary history of Taiwan's comfort women that TWRF released in 2005 entitled *Silent Scars: History of Sexual Slavery by the Japanese Military – A Pictorial Book* (2005),[83] TWRF, like its counterpart the Korean Council, strongly criticized Japan for failing to accept responsibility for the comfort women system and its cruel and inhumane treatment of the system's victims:

> When will Japan bear its responsibility as Germany had done? We demand that Japan, forever flaunting the image of a civilized nation, honestly accept its responsibility and act expeditiously to win back trust and respect from the international community.[84]

At other times as well, TWRF has been equally critical. In 1995 when Japan's quasi-official AWF proposed a ¥2 million (approximately $18,000) "atonement" payment to every surviving comfort woman, TWRF joined the Korean Council in opposing this. Because neither the acceptance of responsibility nor the proposed payments were from official government sources, TWRF maintained that "not a single Taiwanese victim accepted the 'compensation' from the Asian Women's Fund." For its part, the Taiwanese government itself provided a payment of an equivalent amount to each surviving Taiwanese comfort woman.[85] It also extended a monthly subsidy of $15,000 TWD (Taiwanese Dollars), approximately $550 U.S. Dollars, to each of the surviving women.[86] The funds were described as an advance to the women by the Taiwanese government. The government anticipated that these funds would eventually be returned to Taiwan by Japan once a final settlement was

---

[82] "Projects by Country or Region-Taiwan," Asian Women's Fund, http://www.awf.or.jp/e3/taiwan.html.
[83] Lai et al., *Silent Scars*, 193.
[84] Lai et al., *Silent Scars*, 29.
[85] Lai et al., *Silent Scars*, 102.
[86] Lai et al., *Silent Scars*.

reached.[87] In addition to Taiwanese government funds, individual donors in Taiwan also provided support to the victims.[88] Immediately after the ill-fated December 28, 2015 settlement between the governments of Korea and Japan, Taiwanese President Ma Ying-jeou called upon Japan to not limit itself to Korea, but to also address the case of Taiwan's comfort women through a similar official apology and compensation.[89]

Some statements in TWRF's *Silent Scars: History of Sexual Slavery by the Japanese Military – A Pictorial Book* caused the organization to be viewed as a tool of the KMT, due to making public the Taiwanese who had collaborated with the Japanese government. It described how some Taiwanese and Koreans had done the bidding of the Japanese military by rounding up comfort women:

While Japanese *amnesia* has sought to wipe out comfort women, Japan's Asian neighbors in some cases, may have failed to look inward. A number of abductors of comfort women were Korean and Taiwanese. [90]

TWRF also portrayed President Li Teng-hui, Taiwan's first native-born Taiwanese President, as "pro-Japanese," pointing out that he "flaunted his defiance of anti-Japanese Taiwanese by posing as a samurai in one notorious photograph."[91]

Today the TWRF has new, younger leadership who recognize that efforts to memorialize and seek justice for Taiwan's comfort women require more finesse than frontal assaults on Japan. TWRF's Executive Director Kang Shu-hua, who holds a master's degree in Social Work from Columbia University, has learned to detect and navigate the landmines of Taiwan's political and diplomatic landscape. She understands that most Taiwanese rely on Japan's support to retain, as 96% of the citizens of Taiwan wish,[92] a political identity and trajectory independent from China's.

---

[87] "Comfort Women Tell Japan to Extend Compensation," *BBC News*, December 29, 2015, http://www.bbc.com/news/world-asia-35193432.
[88] Lai et al., *Silent Scars*, 102.
[89] Mark Carnac, "Taiwan Urges Japan to Apologize for 'Comfort Women' after South Korean Deal," *Time*, December 29, 2015, http://time.com/4164004/taiwan-japan-comfort-women-resolution/.
[90] Lai et al., *Silent Scars*, 3.
[91] Lai et al., *Silent Scars*.
[92] "Ratio Identifying as Taiwanese Highest in 20 years: Poll," *The China Post*, March 15, 2016, http://www.chinapost.com.tw/taiwan/national/national-news/2016/03/15/460817/ratio-identifying.htm.

Cultural, humanitarian, and defense partnerships serve to deepen and preserve bilateral relations with Japan, which remains Taiwan's second largest trading partner.[93] Prime Minister Abe, frustrated by Beijing's ongoing ventures in military brinkmanship, has sent signals that Japan could opt to use force if China initiated military operations against Taiwan.[94] That statement of support alone might explain why 65% of Taiwanese either feel "close or very close" to Japan[95] and why TWRF's past strident attacks on sympathetic views towards Japan have been curtailed.

In October 2016, Academia Sinica's Institute of Modern History resident senior scholar, Dr. Shiu Wen-Tang, and I met with the TWRF Executive Director Kang Shu-hua,[96] who elaborated on ways in which the handling of the comfort women issue in Taiwan remains politically sensitive. When we inquired about whether TWRF might set up a comfort women statue near the new Ama Museum for Taiwan's comfort women, one of her staff members confided that overseas groups had offered to fund such a statue but that TWRF declined to accept. TWRF representatives expressed concern that the statue would provoke a backlash, including the possible defacement of the statue by pro-Japan Taiwanese groups who would view this as a calculated "impairment" of Japan's "dignity."[97]

In October 2015, Taiwanese President and KMT party leader Ma Ying-jeou called upon citizens of Taiwan to first remember the good that Japan had done for Taiwan "while not forgetting the bad."[98] TWRF obviously does not forget the bad. At the same time, unlike the Korean Council, TWRF has a broader institutional mandate than the comfort women issue. Prior to being chosen by Taiwan's legislative Yuan to oversee comfort women matters in Taiwan, TWRF, which was founded in 1987, focused on addressing childhood prostitution and assisting its victims. When it assumed responsibility in 1992 for seeking justice for Taiwan's comfort women, the TWRF chose not to abandon its work with children. It views the comfort women experience as a resource to inform TWRF work in its other areas of activity.[99]

---

[93] Michal Thim and Misato Matsuoka, "The Odd Couple: Japan & Taiwan's Unlikely Friendship," The Diplomat, May 15, 2014, http://thediplomat.com/2014/05/the-odd-couple-japan-taiwans-unlikely-friendship/.
[94] Thim and Matsuoka, "The Odd Couple: Japan & Taiwan's Unlikely Friendship."
[95] Thim and Matsuoka, "The Odd Couple: Japan & Taiwan's Unlikely Friendship."
[96] Ms. Shu-hua Kang (executive director, Taiwan Women's Rescue Foundation), in discussion with the author, October 24, 2016.
[97] Ministry of Foreign Affairs of Japan, "Announcement by Foreign Ministers."
[98] "Taiwan President Says," Reuters.
[99] "About TWRF," Taipei Women's Rescue Foundation, https://www.twrf.org.tw/eng/p1-about.php.

TWRF committed itself to establishing a site to commemorate Taiwan's comfort women in 2004.[100] It finally opened the Ama (Grandmother) Museum in December 2016 after many challenges. The Museum has two exhibition halls. The first hall displays photos and images that convey information about the comfort women system that Japan created. It exposes its depravity and the suffering that the women endured and the "trauma faced by survivors."[101] The survivors, nevertheless, are "the stars of the show" and are "cast not as the powerless victims of a monumental atrocity, but instead as leading figures in their own human rights struggle," that is, the struggle to press the Japanese government for an official apology and compensation.[102] This pursuit of redress is the theme of the museum's second exhibition hall. It depicts the survivors "leading protest marches or attending legal proceedings in Japan."[103] Kang explains: "These victims want their reputation and dignity to be restored. That can only arise from the Japanese government adopting a truly reflective attitude on this topic."[104]

The TWRF website also depicts the full lives of the comfort women, both their suffering and their triumphs, including their participation in a variety of cultural activities including art and dance.[105] TWRF has worked, Kang observes, to help the former comfort women to gain the confidence to "stand up for themselves and find their voice."[106] When the first comfort women came forward, they spoke from behind a curtain; that initial reserve changed as they found and learned to support each other. Kang compares the comfort women to today's victims of sexual and domestic violence that TWRF supports: "A lot of people are just like these Ama in that they don't want society to know what happened to them." She adds, "So we think that through the courage and strength of these Ama, we can encourage others to speak up."[107]

Keith Menconi, an independent journalist and radio host in Taiwan, did report on the Museum in April 2017. His visit led him to conclude that "the real aim of the Ama Museum is to humanize the survivors and draw attention to their

---

[100] "[Press Release] Opening Ceremony—Royal Family Peace and Women's Human Rights Museum," Taipei Women's Rescue Foundation, December 12, 2016, http://www.twrf.org.tw/amamuseum/news_d9.php.

[101] Keith Menconi, "Lives of Resilience: Reimagining Taiwan's Comfort Women," The News Lens, April 21, 2017, https://international.thenewslens.com/article/66537.

[102] Menconi, "Lives of Resilience: Reimagining Taiwan's Comfort Women."

[103] Menconi, "Lives of Resilience: Reimagining Taiwan's Comfort Women."

[104] Menconi, "Lives of Resilience: Reimagining Taiwan's Comfort Women."

[105] To see how the TWRF depicts the lives of the comfort women, see their website at http://www.twrf.org.tw/amamuseum/index.php and a video published by the TWRF at https://www.youtube.com/watch?v=2nijJEEm7SU.

[106] Menconi, "Lives of Resilience."

[107] Menconi, "Lives of Resilience."

lifetime of resilience.[108] TWRF's approach calls upon visitors to consider what this past history "has to do with their lives and the world we are living in today."[109] It could have applications for Korean and Korean-American supporters of the comfort women cause. Korean and Korean-American organizations tend to focus largely, if not exclusively, on memorializing the comfort women's tragic suffering and on Japan's culpability in creating the comfort women system. However, they do not stress how the comfort women coming forward can encourage today's victims of human trafficking and domestic violence to come forward as well. Ironically, still today Korea[110] and Japan[111] number among the developed countries that fare worst in addressing domestic violence. These two countries are also cited for ongoing major involvement in human trafficking.[112][113]

In the Taiwan equation for survival, close ties with Japan remain a critical component. The current Taiwanese government and TWRF can thus be expected to continue to address the comfort women issue with more deference to Japan than in Korea. Statements of support for Taiwan by Japan's Prime Minister Abe, including his bold April 2013 decision to support the sharing of fishing rights with Taiwan around the disputed Senkaku Islands[114] and his deliberate reference to Taiwan in his April 2015 speech to a Joint Session of the United States Congress,[115] afford Taiwan a needed morale boost and political leverage for the present and the near future. While some harbor grievances related to Taiwan's colonial past, the vast majority of

---

[108] Menconi, "Lives of Resilience."
[109] Menconi, "Lives of Resilience."
[110] John Power, "[Voice] Is Domestic Violence Taken Seriously in Korea?" *The Korea Herald*, May 5, 2012, http://www.koreaherald.com/view.php?ud=20120507001291.
[111] Rob Gilhooly, "Learning to Stand up to Domestic Violence in Japan," *Japan Times*, March 4, 2017, http://www.japantimes.co.jp/news/2017/03/04/national/social-issues/learning-stand-domestic-violence-japan/#.WPzav_k1-Uk.
[112] Dan Lamothe, "'The U.S. Military's Long, Uncomfortable History with Prostitution Gets New Attention," *Washington Post*, October 31, 2014, https://www.washingtonpost.com/news/checkpoint/wp/2014/10/31/the-u-s-militarys-long-uncomfortable-history-with-prostitution-gets-new-attention/?utm_term=.f1fda4b218d1.
[113] Sandy Cameron and Edward Newman, "Trafficking of Filipino Women to Japan: Examining the Experiences and Perspectives of Victims and Experts" (executive summary, prepared for Global Programme against Trafficking in Persons, United Nations University, 2004), 3, http://www.unodc.org/pdf/crime/human_trafficking/Exec_summary_UNU.pdf.
[114] Yabuki Susumu and Mark Selden, "The Origins of the Senkaku/Diaoyu Dispute between China, Taiwan and Japan," *The Asia-Pacific Journal* 12, no. 2 (January 2014): 1–25, http://apjjf.org/2014/12/2/Yabuki-Susumu/4061/article.html.
[115] Shinzo Abe, "'Towards an Alliance of Hope'—Address to a Joint Meeting of the U.S. Congress" (speech, Washington D.C., United States, April 29, 2015), available at http://japan.kantei.go.jp/97_abe/statement/201504/uscongress.html.

Taiwanese have gone beyond those sentiments.[116] Unlike China and Korea, they refuse to allow Taiwan's comfort women issue to metamorphose into "a righteous battle against Japan."[117]

---

[116] Thim and Masuoka, "The Odd Couple."
[117] Soh, *The Comfort Women,* 22–23.

8

Statue Politics vs. East Asian Security: The Growing Role of China and Chinese-American Civil Society

Beijing's Position on the Comfort Women Controversy

While small towns in the United States are being pulled into the comfort women feud between Korea and Japan, China has made it manifestly clear that it intends to become the new sheriff in the Asia-Pacific region, edging out the United States. It is confronting American sea and air power in the South China Sea and through its new Air Defense Identification Zone (ADIZ) in Northeast Asia. While the United States should not seek to thwart China's legitimate development, neither should it passively stand by and allow disunity among its allies to create a leadership vacuum that an increasingly militaristic and Marxist-inspired China could fill. This would not serve the interests of those who wish China to progress through embracing the rule of law, opting to resolve problems through negotiation and compromise rather than through brinkmanship. Further breakdowns in Korea-Japan relations and perhaps even in U.S.-Japan relations due to inflammatory rhetoric on memorials in small American municipalities and in Congressional resolutions, based exclusively on a Korean account of events that inspires anti-Japanese sentiments, are a cause for concern. In addition to geographic proximity to China and a bilateral volume of trade that exceeds Korea's cumulative trade with Japan and the United States, Korea and China share a deep-seated hostility towards Japan, stemming largely from unresolved WWII issues.[1] Relations between the Republic of Korea and China have deepened since the 1980s, leading some to foresee an eventual alliance between the two countries.[2]

---

[1] Soh, *The Comfort Women*, 22–23.
[2] Jin Kai, "Why a China-South Korea Alliance Won't Happen," The Diplomat, August

In San Francisco's Chinatown, a WWII Pacific War Memorial Hall opened on August 15, 2015, commemorating the 70th anniversary of the "Chinese People's War of Resistance against Japanese Aggression."[3] Michael Honda, the unflagging U.S. Congressional proponent of a more assertive Japanese apology, was named "Honorary Curator" of the museum.[4] The *China Daily* quotes Florence Fang, a key figure in the creation of the museum:

> The Jewish people and community have established 167 monuments and museums worldwide to memorize the holocaust against Jews. We didn't even have one to commemorate the contribution and sacrifice of the Chinese people, even though the death toll of Chinese in WWII was 36 million.[5]

The organization spearheading the museum is the Global Alliance for Preserving the History of WWII in Asia. The opening line of its mission statement echoes the Chinese Communist Party in denouncing Japan and asserting that "a full accounting for the Asia-Pacific War is imperative when ruling elements of the Japanese government foster collective amnesia and ultra-nationalistic citizens engage in denial, justification and whitewashing of Japanese war crimes committed in the first half of the 20th century."[6]

Unlike China, Japan and Korea have fully embraced democracy and the rule of law, with its concomitant attributes of accountability, transparency and accessible, and impartial dispute resolution.[7] U.S.-Korea-Japan cooperation is critically important, especially as China's "peaceful rise" exhibits a still tenuous commitment to the rule of law and to the peaceful settlement of regional disputes. The world was reminded of this a few years back when a *People's Daily* editorial warned that if Hong Kong's "Occupy Central" disruptions continued, "consequences will be unimaginable,"[8] which could be

---

20, 2014, http://thediplomat.com/2014/08/why-a-china-south-korea-alliance-wont-happen/.

[3] Chang Jun, "Chinese WWII Museum Names Mike Honda Honorary Curator," *China Daily*, March 2, 2015, http://www.chinadaily.com.cn/world/2015-03/02/content_19755364.htm.

[4] Jun, "Chinese WWII Museum Names Mike Honda Honorary Curator."

[5] Jun, "Chinese WWII Museum Names Mike Honda Honorary Curator."

[6] "Our Mission," Global Alliance, http://www.global-alliance.net/mission.html. See also Zachary Keck, "China's Communist Party and Japan: A Forgotten History," *The National Interest*, May 27, 2014, http://nationalinterest.org/feature/chinas-communist-party-japan-forgotten-history-10533?page=2.

[7] See, e.g., World Justice Project, https://worldjusticeproject.org/about-us/overview/what-rule-law.

[8] See "Cherish Positive Growth: Defend Hong Kong's Prosperity and Stability,"

interpreted as either a warning of socioeconomic collapse or of a potential Tiananmen-style military crackdown. Fortunately both were avoided, hopefully affirming that all sides have learned from the tragedy of a quarter century past. Nevertheless, it remains unclear whether sufficient guarantees are in place to assure that the politics of modern China be guided by the rule of law rather than by Mao's "barrel of a gun."[9] As we have already stated, Beijing has recently detained not only human rights activists but also the attorneys who dare to defend them.[10] [11] China's attitude towards civil and human rights will be influenced by the U.S.-Japan-Korea working relationship and the ability of these three countries to convince China to opt for rule of law rather than the dictates of the Chinese Communist Party in addressing problems at home as well as with its neighbors.

Beijing and the Comfort Woman Issue: Pretender, Friend or Foe?

Until now, comfort women memorials have been placed in smaller cities with populations of less than 150,000. In September 2017, San Francisco became the first major U.S. city to install a comfort women memorial.[12] Supporters forged ahead with plans to install a comfort women memorial in an extension to St. Mary's Square in Chinatown. Although they obtained the approval of political decision-makers, their plans conflicted with the prior agreement of the developer of the site to delegate the selection of artwork there to the nonprofit Chinese Cultural Center with community input. Out of 100 artists worldwide, the piece selected by the community-based group was by Chinese-American artist Sarah Sze. The developer and Sze began working on artwork for the site, but when Sze learned that the comfort women activists had obtained political approval for their statue in the small space, she withdrew her project. The activists later pleaded that they "did not barge in," and argued curiously that Sze was only a Chinese-American artist but that the comfort women memorial addressed issues related to "Asian-American women in general." The artist director of the Chinese Cultural Center lamented that "politics

---

People's Daily Editorial, October 1, 2014, as translated by Nikhil Sonnad, "Here is the Full Text of the Chinese Communist Party's Message to Hong Kong," *Quartz*, October 01, 2014, http://qz.com/274425/here-is-the-full-text-of-the-chinese-communist-partys-message-to-hong-kong/.

[9] Mao Tse Tung, "Quotations from Mao Tse Tung," trans. David Quentin and Brian Baggins, Marxists Internet Archive, https://www.marxists.org/reference/archive/mao/works/red-book/ch05.htm.

[10] "Trial of Lawyer," *Taipei Times*.

[11] Gregory, "Human Rights Lawyers Shine in China," *The Epoch Times*.

[12] "San Francisco Unveils 'Comfort Women' Memorial," *Japan Times*, September 23, 2017, https://www.japantimes.co.jp/news/2017/09/23/national/politics-diplomacy/san-francisco-unveils-comfort-women-memorial/#.Wc66DVvWyUl.

trumped the community process."[13]

Beijing: Vocal on Japan and Mum on Mao

In October 2016, with the help of monies donated from South Korea, a monument which includes both a Korean comfort woman and a Chinese comfort woman was dedicated in Shanghai Normal University.[14] It attracted significant publicity including an exchange of opprobrium between the foreign ministries of Japan and the People's Republic of China. When Japan's Chief Cabinet Secretary and official spokesperson Yoshihide Suga characterized the establishment of the memorial as "extremely regrettable," China's Foreign Ministry retorted, calling for a similar memorial in Tokyo to "help Japan unload the burden of history and win the understanding of Asian neighbors."[15]

However, 2016 did not only mark the creation of the first comfort women memorial in China; it marked the 50th anniversary of the start of Mao's Cultural Revolution. While the comfort women statues were deemed of sufficient importance to warrant a defense by China's Ministry of Foreign Affairs,[16] China maintained a guarded silence on the Cultural Revolution throughout 2016. Interestingly, 2016 marked both the 50th anniversary of the beginning of the Cultural Revolution and 40th anniversary of it being halted with the arrest of the Gang of Four shortly after Mao's death in September 1976. Yet there was no monument dedicated to the victims of the Cultural Revolution, which turned children on parents and claimed hundreds of thousands of lives and resulted in the persecution of "100 million people." Yet in 2016 there was no ceremony to mourn those victims. There was no state expression of regret for Mao who had rained death and a decade-long nightmare of terror upon his fellow countrymen.[17] Certainly in the decade following Mao's death in September 1976 there were significant efforts by the

---

[13] Joshua Sabatini, "'Comfort Women' Memorial Costs SF Major Art Project," San Francisco Examiner, December 28, 2016, http://www.sfexaminer.com/comfort-women-memorial-costs-sf-major-art-project/.

[14] "'Comfort Women' Statues Erected in China," Yonhap News Agency, October 22, 2016, http://english.yonhapnews.co.kr/news/2016/10/22/34/0200000000AEN20161022001851315F.html.

[15] "China Prods Japan to Erect 'Comfort Women' Statue in Tokyo," ABS-CBN News, October 25, 2016, http://news.abs-cbn.com/overseas/10/25/16/china-prods-japan-to-erect-comfort-women-statue-in-tokyo

[16] "Foreign Ministry Spokesperson Lu Kang's Regular Press Conference on October 25, 2016," Ministry of Foreign Affairs of the People's Republic of China, October 25, 2016, http://www.fmprc.gov.cn/mfa_eng/xwfw_665399/s2510_665401/t1408663.shtml.

[17] Thomas J. Ward, "Remembering the Chinese Spring," Washington Times, December 27, 2016, https://www.washingtontimes.com/news/2016/dec/27/remembering-the-chinese-spring/.

Chinese government to rectify the wrongdoings of the Cultural Revolution that all ended with the Tiananmen Square crackdown, which claimed another thousand lives.

One questions the sincerity and extent of China's concern for human rights. While China memorializes the several hundred thousand comfort women, there exists no monument to the victims of the Cultural Revolution. There is also no monument in China to the tens of millions of victims of Mao's Great Leap Forward. In a 2010 *New York Times* editorial, Frank Dikötter, a Dutch sinologist who has studied Mao's rule of China, reported on his review of hundreds of official documents surrounding Mao's Great Leap Forward, which took place from 1958 to 1962. The Great Leap Forward was intended to launch China as a model for agricultural and industrial development but proved to be a colossal failure. Dikötter concluded, based on his document review, that the number of deaths during the Great Leap Forward has been downplayed by the Chinese government. He cites the example of his findings in Sichuan Province where one official submitted an uncontested report to the local communist leader Li Jingquan that, in Sichuan alone, 10.6 million people had perished between 1958 and 1961. Dikötter then makes the observation that "in all, the records I studied suggest that the Great Leap Forward was responsible for at least 45 million deaths." [18]

He stresses that his examination of party records confirms that the Great Leap Forward was not the product of clumsy errors in the government of Chairman Mao, as has been suggested, and that coercion and terror were at the very core of its implementation. Dikötter cites unimaginable acts of cruelty such as the dismembering of people and or being buried alive or drowned as punishment for "crimes" such as "digging up a potato" or taking a handful of grain. And Dikötter maintains that Mao was aware of these tragedies:

> Mao was sent many reports about what was happening in the countryside, some of them scribbled in longhand. He knew about the horror, but pushed for even greater extractions of food. At a secret meeting in Shanghai on March 25, 1959, he ordered the party to procure up to one-third of all the available grain – much more than ever before. The minutes of the meeting reveal a chairman insensitive to human loss: "when there is not enough to eat people starve to death. It is better to let half of the people die so that the other half can eat their fill."[19]

---

[18] Frank Dikötter, "Mao's Great Leap to Famine," *New York Times*, December 15, 2010, http://www.nytimes.com/2010/12/16/opinion/16iht-eddikotter16.html?_r=2.
[19] Dikötter, "Mao's Great Leap to Famine."

The Black Book of Communism succinctly describes how the deification of Mao and the party defied any pretense of a system of justice: "In China, people were not arrested because they were guilty; they were guilty because they had been arrested."[20] Yet none of this merits a memorial in China. Does the comfort women memorial honor the women or does it simply feed on China's competition with Japan in the Pacific?

China's Modern-Day Comfort Women System Using North Korean Women and Girls

While Korean and Korean-American CSOs collaborate with Beijing-related organizations in the United States in erecting statues to honor the comfort women, they remain mysteriously silent about a phenomenon occurring today in China with young women from North Korea. Tens of thousands of young Korean women have fled the North by crossing the Yalu River into China. They do so with the help of Chinese "coyotes" who bring them to the Chinese mainland for high fees. The fees can be immediately paid by cash or can be paid off once the escapee arrives in China. Frequently, these young women find themselves channeled into prostitution upon arrival in China. Those sent to brothels are deceived in the same way that the "comfort women" were some 80 years ago. Like the comfort women of that period, they are promised work as barmaids or as servers to pay those who smuggled them into China, only to discover that a life of forced prostitution awaits them. Hyeon-seo Lee, a North Korean refugee who escaped to China in the late 1990s, was forced into a marriage and, when the marriage failed, was sold to a brothel which she was fortunate to escape. Her book, *The Girl with Seven Names* (2015), relates the twisted course she endured to reach Seoul, where she now speaks out against the repression in North Korea and the trafficking of North Korean women in China. Ms. Lee has established an NGO called North Star NK designed to help those trafficked into the sex trade in China to escape. She describes the fate of the "humiliated and broken" women forced into the Chinese underworld:

> All but the lucky few will live the rest of their lives in utter misery. They will be repeatedly raped day in and day out by an endless supply of customers who enrich their captors at their expense.[21]

---

[20] Jean-Louis Margolin, "China: A Long March into Night", in *The Black Book of Communism: Crimes, Terror, Repression,* ed. Stéphane Courtois, trans. Jonathan Murphy and Mark Kramer (Cambridge, MA: Harvard University Press, 1999), 507.
[21] "Lottery of Misery: Bleak Choices for N Korean Women," *Taipei Times*, November 4, 2016, http://www.taipeitimes.com/News/world/archives/2016/11/04/2003658564.

The trafficking of North Korean women has grown since the North Korean famine of the 1990s. One victim, Park Ji-hyun, explains that "human trafficking of North Koreans to China, especially women who will be dispatched to brothels, has become big business."[22] Park was sold to a Chinese man, lived as his spouse for six years, and gave birth to one child. She then escaped only to be captured and was detained in a camp for North Korean women who had been trafficked and captured in China. The women were forced each day in the first week of detention to strip before male prison guards who inspected their vaginal and rectal cavities for money. They were finally deported back to North Korea where Park was held in a concentration camp for six months. Once released, she again returned to China to find her son. Ms. Park describes it this way:

> People just like me – women fleeing a brutal dictatorship, only to be trafficked to a cruel one – are leading lives of perpetual victimization, utterly powerless. Unless the world pays attention, they will remain without protection – and without hope.[23]

One would hope that organizations such as the KAFC and the Korean Council for the Women Drafted for Military Sexual Slavery by Japan would use their influence to speak out forcefully on behalf of these women who face no choice but life-threatening repression in North Korea or the dangers of forced marriages or sexual slavery upon fleeing to China. One would hope that they would lobby China to allow these women to travel to Seoul rather than to repatriate them to the North as is the current practice.

Korean-American CSOs and Pro-Beijing Organizations: The New Partnership

In 2015, Chinese-American CSOs played the pivotal role in gaining approval of a comfort women memorial in San Francisco's Chinatown. Two retired Chinese-American judges, Julie Tang and Lillian Sing of the "Rape of Nanking" Redress Coalition[24] have also assumed leadership roles in the "Comfort Women" Justice Coalition,[25] a second anti-Japan initiative which focuses on redress from Japan for the comfort women. The campaigns against Japan for its crimes in Nanjing (Nanking) and for the creation of the

---

[22] Park Ji-hyun, "Surviving Human Trafficking in the PRC," *Taipei Times,* August 23, 2016, http://www.taipeitimes.com/News/editorials/archives/2016/08/23/2003653672.
[23] Ji-hyun, "Surviving Human Trafficking in the PRC."
[24] "History," Rape of Nanking Redress Coalition, http://rnrc-us.org/history.htm.
[25] "'Comfort Women' Panel Discussion at UC Hastings College," Comfort Women Justice Coalition, http://remembercomfortwomen.org.

comfort station system are understandable; however, the absence of a Great Leap Forward Redress Coalition, a Cultural Revolution Redress Coalition, or a Tiananmen Square Truth Commission points to perilous one-sidedness in this campaign for human rights where Japan is punished and Maoist acts of repression and mass murder are ignored.

Korean-American CSOs that work with pro-Beijing organizations to build more anti-Japan monuments should understand that young North Korean women arrive in China every week to escape the oppression and madness of Pyongyang. While these young women expect to work as servers and restaurant workers, some will be sold as brides upon their arrival to unmarried, often older Chinese men who could not find a spouse. Others will go to the "restaurant or café" where they expect to be servers, only to find themselves in brothels instead where they work as "comfort women." There are 20,000 to 30,000 North Korean women in China who currently face this tragic fate.[26]

Comfort Women versus China's Female Victims of Japan's Imperial Army

Many women in mainland China suffered abduction, rape, and murder at the hands of the Japanese military prior to and during WWII. In October 2015 a monument, which included statues of a Chinese comfort woman and a Korean comfort woman seated beside each other, was erected in Seoul, ostensibly to recall the shared fate of the two countries.[27] In October 2016 a similar monument was dedicated in China.[28] In her study of what she refers to as Chinese "comfort women," Prof. Peipei Qiu, a literature professor at Vassar College, writes of the tragic circumstances that thousands of Chinese women suffered under Japan's military.[29]

Japan's official, government-sanctioned comfort women were channeled through the Ministry of War. They consisted of Japanese, Korean, and

---

[26] Donald Kirk, "North Korean Women Sold into 'Slavery' in China," *Christian Science Monitor,* May 11, 2012, https://www.csmonitor.com/World/Asia-Pacific/2012/0511/North-Korean-women-sold-into-slavery-in-China.
[27] "Statues Honoring Korean, Chinese 'Comfort Women' Erected in Seoul," *Japan Times,* October 29, 2015, http://www.japantimes.co.jp/news/2015/10/29/national/politics-diplomacy/statues-honoring-korean-chinese-comfort-women-erected-in-seoul/.
[28] "'Comfort Women' Statues Erected in China," *Yonhap News Agency*, October 22, 2016, http://english.yonhapnews.co.kr/news/2016/10/22/34/0200000000AEN20161022001851315F.html.
[29] Peipei Qiu, Su Zhiliang, and Chen Lifei, *Chinese Comfort Women: Testimonies from Imperial Japan's Sex Slaves* (New York: Oxford University Press, 2014), 26–28.

Taiwanese women, all subjects of Japan, and were conscripted to curb the rape and mistreatment of Asian females in newly conquered territories. These three populations were considered trustworthy because they were subjects of the emperor and thought to be fulfilling a necessary, honorable task through their role as comfort women.[30]

Unlike Taiwanese and Korean women, Chinese women were not subjects of Japan. They did not warrant trust or an assumption of patriotism toward Japan, especially given China's massive resistance to Japan's occupation of the mainland. The Chinese women forced into sexual service by local Japanese military units were viewed instead as "spoils of war," similar to the Bosnian Muslim women raped and murdered by the Serbs in the 1990s and the Nigerian girls who were kidnapped, raped, and murdered in more recent times by the terror group Boko Haram.

Beijing's Gains from the Proliferation of Comfort Women Memorials in the United States

New efforts to advance the comfort women narrative in the United States increasingly originate from Chinese-American CSOs. The Chinese denounce Japan's creation of a system that had no place for Chinese women because they were viewed as a security threat. China's anti-Japanese CSOs' goals in jumping on the official comfort women bandwagon are arguably strategic. By supporting and partnering with Korean CSOs and promoting their anti-Japan position, they help to support the growing divide in inter-state relations between Japan and Korea, which serves to undermine the Korea-U.S.-Japan strategic alliance.

---

[30] Tanaka, *Japan's Comfort Women*, 3.

9

Inconsistencies in the Korean Narrative

Korea's Self-Exoneration

After WWII, allied tribunals convicted numerous Koreans of participation in war crimes. More recently, however, a Korean group called the "Truth Commission on Forced Mobilization under Japanese Imperialism," formed under Korean President Roh Moo-hyun, examined those convictions and announced on November 13, 2006, that "83 of the 146 Koreans convicted of war crimes were victims of Japan and should not be blamed." Michael Breen, *Korea Times* contributor and author of the popular text *The Koreans* (2004) reacted critically. Breen pointed out that the international tribunals that rendered the convictions had reached their judgments based on a review of the available evidence, and persons who were merely doing their jobs were acquitted. As to those convicted, Breen comments:

> They were not tried as soldiers or POW camp guards who had done their jobs. They were tried for overzealousness, for decisions and actions over and above the call of duty. They were the thugs, the brutes, the monsters, the most horrible…

Breen describes atrocities committed by Korean camp guards that represented indignities that no human being should suffer. He chastised the commission for its political correctness: "The Commission should know that those rounding up comfort women were Koreans and those torturing people in police stations were mostly Koreans." He added that "people who committed crimes against humanity are not innocent by virtue of being Korean any more than Japanese who brutalized Koreans are innocent by virtue of being Japanese."

Breen's father had a close friend who had been a prisoner of war and suffered under Korean guards. Breen offers poignant insight into the only path to genuine clemency and rebuked the Korean officials who reversed the convictions of Korea's war criminals:

> So Truth Commissioners, who's the victim, my father's friend or the camp guard? Ultimately we can say with distance that both were. But there is a process to get there. First the criminal must acknowledge his crimes, and only then can he be forgiven. The Truth Commission had no right to intervene in the process and forgive Korean war criminals. That is for their victims to do. How many of their stories has the Commission examined? As it goes about addressing issues from the Japanese period, modern Korea owes it to the victims – in this case, the prisoners brutalized by those convicted war criminals – to tread with sensitivity on their graves.[1]

The Truth Commission's handling of convicted war criminals of Korean ethnicity is in stark contrast with the way in which the United States and Europe treat alleged non-German Nazi war criminals even today. It does not matter if such individuals were or were not German nationals. Innocence or guilt is determined based on an examination of facts. John Demjanjuk, a naturalized American citizen of Ukrainian descent, was stripped of his U.S. citizenship and deported first to Israel and then to Germany for alleged war crimes. He spent the final decade of his life in courts until his death in 2012 without a definitive resolution of his guilt or innocence for crimes he allegedly committed as a very young man. Should Demjanjuk have been pre-emptively declared innocent because he was not an ethnic German and a victim of what the Korean Truth Commission referred to as "forced mobilization" because Germans Nazis forced him to function as a prison guard?

Another example of selective exoneration involves the post-WWII continuation of a Korean comfort women system for the benefit of the U.S. military. Little is said of the social attitudes and financial expediencies in Korea that made it possible that "for more than 50 years after the Korean War, hundreds of thousands of young South Korean women continued to endure sexual exploitation and violence as they labored in camp towns serving the U.S. military."[2]

---

[1] Michael Breen, "Truth Commission Should Be Truthful," *Korea Times*, November 16, 2006, http://sakuramochi-jp.blogspot.com/2012/05/truth-commission-should-be-truthful.html.

[2] Soh, *The Comfort Women*, xvi.

The Korean Role in the Recruitment and Conscription of Comfort Women

Yuki Tanaka also points out that Koreans acted as subcontractors for the Japanese comfort women procurers in WWII and "targeted young daughters of poor peasant families, knowing that it was relatively easy to trick them"[3] and that "many young women were sold to brothels in return for an advance payment to their families."[4] Tanaka cites an article that appeared in the *Dong-ah Ilbo* newspaper in September 1927 with the headline "Poverty makes prostitutes," recognizing that Korea's economic and social conditions were pushing some young Korean females to prostitution.[5]

Tanaka maintains that Koreans were not only involved in the recruitment of women but also in the management of the comfort stations themselves. He gives the example of the city of Jiujiang in China's Jiangxi Province, where "16 comfort stations opened in 1940 and half of these newly opened comfort stations, and two of the restaurants, were run by Korean proprietors."[6] Tanaka adds that "by the early stages of the Asia-Pacific War many Japanese and Korean proprietors who had been operating prostitution businesses in Korea had moved to China due to economic problems in the colony and had started operating there for the Japanese troops and the military's civilian employees."[7]

C. Sarah Soh charges that "[f]ew are willing to consider the unsavory fact that, accustomed to 'customary' public institutions that grant men a sex-right to satisfy their carnal desires outside matrimony, few Koreans opposed, and many collaborated in recruiting and running comfort stations by trafficking girls and young women."[8] Testimonies from the Korean comfort women themselves also confirm that Koreans participated in the recruitment of comfort women.[9] Soh further maintains that "Koreans actually outnumbered civilian Japanese among those seeking profit by human trafficking, forcing prostitution and sexual slavery upon young female compatriots."[10] Soh feels that the Korean redress movement allegedly supporting the comfort women lost its bearing. Instead of defending and standing up for the female victims, the movement has allowed the cause of the comfort women to be supplanted

---

[3] Tanaka, *Japan's Comfort Women*, 38.
[4] Tanaka, *Japan's Comfort Women*, 35.
[5] Tanaka, *Japan's Comfort Women*, 27
[6] Tanaka, *Japan's Comfort Women*, 37.
[7] Tanaka, *Japan's Comfort Women*, 37.
[8] Soh, *The Comfort Women*, 224.
[9] Howard, *True Stories*, 81, 89, 96, 106.
[10] Soh, *The Comfort Women*, 139–140.

by Korean nationalism. Soh is sharply critical of the politicized rhetoric used by an American in one major report on the comfort women and states that "categorically defining the Japanese comfort stations as 'rape centers' – as the United Nations special rapporteur Gay McDougall did – is a political act in support of the redress movement".[11]

Tanaka and Soh both point to a variety of factors that support the view that the current Korean narrative has been co-opted in favor of Korean nationalism. The denialists on the Japan side are also strongly motivated by nationalism rather than justice. Sarah Soh sums up the current debate in the following way:

> ...one nationally and internationally known Japanese feminist scholar has discerningly problematized, from the mid-1990s, the nationalistic discourses in Japan and Korea, that, respectively, represent comfort women either as "willing prostitutes" or "forcibly conscripted virgins," and she has persistently stressed the need for feminism to transcend nationalism. [12]

Soh also reminds her readers that no attention was paid to the comfort women "before the transnational redress movement took off in the 1990s." Rather, they had been largely "marginalized" until that time in both Japan and Korea. [13]

Post-World War II Korean Use of the Comfort Women System?

A comfort women operation was put into place by the Korean military during the Korean War. Soh contends that "[t]he fact that Korean military also availed themselves of the 'special comfort unit' during the Korean War has received little public attention, even since the Korean women's movement in support of the comfort women began in the 1990s."[14] Soh points out that not only Japan but also Korea has had a "long history of similar masculinist sexual mores." [15]

The comfort units that South Korea put in place for its military operated until March 1954[16] or about nine months after the Korean conflict came to an end.

---

[11] Soh, *The Comfort Women*, 235.
[12] Soh, *The Comfort Women*, 237.
[13] Soh, *The Comfort Women*, 224–225.
[14] Soh, *The Comfort Women*, 215
[15] Soh, *The Comfort Women*, 217.
[16] Soh, *The Comfort Women*, 215.

The recruitment of Korean women for this task was justified because "both the imperial Japanese military and the postcolonial Korean army leadership shared the belief in men's uncontrollable need for, and therefore right to, women's bodies outside marriage, whether in war or peace."[17] Soh notes that the Korean comfort unit system largely mirrored the Japanese system, and was equally dehumanizing of women, viewing them as commodities:

> Korean records refer to the women as "fifth category supplies" – an addition to the four normal supply categories, reminiscent of the Japanese classification of women as "military supplies." ... The similarities in the pattern of operations include soldiers lining up in front of the tents, the women being classified according to the ranks of the men they served, and a hierarchical order of access to their sexual services.[18]

U.S. Soldiers and South Korea's "Western Princesses"

When President Park Chung-hee seized power through a military coup in 1961, he initiated a "social purification drive" that included a "prostitution prevention law." However, rather than eliminate prostitution, Park instead created 104 special prostitution districts, being desperate to retain the cash that American soldiers would otherwise spend in Japan.[19] Referred to as "Yankee Princesses" or "Western Princesses," women who worked in these districts were lectured to by Korean university professors, who lauded them for helping to accrue "precious foreign currency for the nation's economic development" and for performing "patriotic" work.[20]

The Korean narrative that American city officials are likely to hear conveniently avoids discussion of the social attitudes and financial expediencies in Korea that made it possible for hundreds of thousands of young South Korean women, for more than 50 years after the Korean War, "to endure sexual exploitation and violence as they labored in camp towns serving the U.S. military."[21] The censored, carefully crafted Korean comfort women narrative that justifies the multiplication of memorials in Korea and in the United States has compromised Korean civil society's advocacy for the victims of the comfort women system. Soh observes:

---

[17] Soh, *The Comfort Women*, 217.
[18] Soh, *The Comfort Women*, 216.
[19] Soh, *The Comfort Women*, 217.
[20] Soh, *The Comfort Women*, 221.
[21] Soh, *The Comfort Women*, xvi.

> It is worth noting here that leaders of South Korea's women's organizations have been galvanized by a strong dose of postcolonial ethnic nationalism and have turned the redress movement into a righteous battle against Japan, demanding truth and justice for the latter's historical wrongdoings perpetrated during its colonial rule.[22]

Koreans have continued until today to procure prostitutes under conditions of near-coercion for the use of their own troops and U.S. servicemen. In 2003, after informal and non-binding hearings instituted by the Philippine government, the Seoul District Court ruled that three night club owners near U.S. Camp Casey must compensate Filipina women who said they had been forced into prostitution at the clubs.[23]

In January 2009, a group of former prostitutes in South Korea accused some of their country's former leaders of encouraging them to have sex with American soldiers, and taking a direct hand in the sex trade from the 1960s through the 1980s, including the building of a testing and treatment system to ensure that the prostitutes were disease-free for the American troops.[24] "Our government was one big pimp for the U.S. military," one of the women, Kim Ae-ran, stated.[25]

Katherine H. S. Moon, a Wellesley College Professor, has written about such prostitution in her 1997 book *Sex Among Allies*. Moon states that there was "active government complicity, support of such camp town prostitution" by both the Korean government and the U.S. military, reflected in minutes of meetings between American military officials and Korean bureaucrats.[26]

The U.S. military presence in both Korea and Japan, and the accompanying violence against women, has generated a multitude of legal actions involving American servicemen. One of the most notorious incidents was widely publicized and fueled anti-U.S. sentiment. Yun Geum-I, a "juicy girl" in a club in Dongducheon, Korea, just outside U.S. Camp Casey, was brutally

---

[22] Soh, *The Comfort Women*, 22–23.
[23] "Court Rules in Favor of Filipina Prostitutes," *Korea JoongAng Daily*, May 31, 2003, http://koreajoongangdaily.joins.com/news/article/article.aspx?aid=1987730.
[24] Choe Sang-hun, "Ex-Prostitutes Say South Korea and U.S. Enabled Sex Trade near Bases," *New York Times*, Jan. 7, 2009, http://www.nytimes.com/2009/01/08/world/asia/08korea.html?pagewanted=2&_r=2&sq=Comfort.
[25] Sang-hun, "Ex-Prostitutes Say South Korea and U.S. Enabled Sex Trade near Bases."
[26] Sang-hun, "Ex-Prostitutes Say South Korea and U.S. Enabled Sex Trade near Bases."

bludgeoned, sodomized with a bottle and an umbrella, and murdered by U.S. Army Private Kenneth L. Markle on October 28, 1991. This particularly vicious crime touched off demonstrations against the U.S. presence in Korea. Markle was initially sentenced to life imprisonment, but his term was reduced to 15 years because Yun's family was compensated by Markle's family and the U.S. government. He was released in 2006.[27] Similarly, the 1995 rape of a 12-year old Okinawan school girl by U.S. Marines sparked public sentiment against the U.S. presence in Japan, where the U.S. military is responsible for a disproportionate number of murders, rapes, and robberies.[28]

In August 1999 police issued an arrest warrant for Kim Kyong Soo, president of the Korean Special Tourism Industry Association, on suspicion that he had brought more than 1,000 Filipina and Russian women into Korea to work as bar girls around U.S. military bases. A judge cancelled the warrant for lack of evidence and closed the case.[29] Nevertheless, an American sergeant told *Time* magazine, in words chillingly similar to the Korean comfort women stories, that the Russian and Filipina women in the Dongducheon bars "are here because they've been tricked. They're told they're going to be bartending or waitressing, but once they get here, things are different."[30] In 2005 a former Filipina bar worker was awarded $5,000 from a South Korean nightclub owner who forced her to have sex with U.S. soldiers for money, and a club owner was convicted of illegal brothel-keeping.[31]

In 2014, 122 former workers in brothels serving American troops in Korea filed suit in the Seoul Central District Court, claiming that the South Korean government controlled their activities and infringed on their human rights against their will.[32] On January 20, 2017, the court partially affirmed their claims, ordering the state to pay five million won each to 57 of the plaintiffs, ruling that the government had no legal basis to forcibly detain them for health reasons in the 1960s and 1970s. However, the court rejected their

---

[27] "U.S. Soldier Free after Brutal 1992 Murder," *Hankyoreh*, October 28, 2006, http://english.hani.co.kr/arti/english_edition/e_national/167869.html.
[28] Andrew Pollack, "Marines Seek Peace with Okinawa in Rape Case," *New York Times*, October 8, 1995, http://www.nytimes.com/1995/10/08/world/marines-seek-peace-with-okinawa-in-rape-case.html?pagewanted=all.
[29] Donald Macintyre, "Base Instincts," *Time*, August 5, 2002, http://content.time.com/time/subscriber/article/0,33009,333899,00.html.
[30] Macintyre, "Base Instincts."
[31] Seth Robson and Hwang Hae-Rym, "Ex-Bar Worker Who Was Forced into Prostitution Wins $5,000 Judgment," *Stars and Stripes*, August 6, 2005, https://www.stripes.com/news/ex-bar-worker-who-was-forced-into-prostitution-wins-5-000-judgment-1.36633#.WRjehxPysUQ.
[32] Larry Alton, "War and Women: The Korean War," CNN Report, December 11, 2014, May 14, 2017, http://ireport.cnn.com/docs/DOC-1196572.

claims that the state violated the law by facilitating prostitution, because they could have exercised their "free will" and not participated.[33]

The Korean military who served in Vietnam has also been singled out for its mistreatment of Vietnamese women. Former U.S. Senator Norm Coleman, who has been associated with an American law firm representing Japanese interests, has called for the South Korean president to publicly apologize for the sexual violence of South Korean troops in Vietnam.[34]

Misogyny in Today's Korea and Japan

Korea and Japan still today number among the countries that have been most criticized for their mistreatment of women. A 1998 front page story in the *New York Times* by Nicholas Kristof entitled "Do Korean Men Still Beat Their Wives? Definitely" highlighted the extent to which spousal abuse by Korean men remained a problem at the very time that the comfort women question had come to the forefront.[35] As recently as 2015 the *Korea Herald* posted a commentary on the "2010 Korea National Survey of Domestic Violence and Sexual Violence." It revealed that some 53.8% of Korean spouses claimed to have suffered some type of violence at the hands of spouses in the year prior to the 2010 questionnaire.[36] The *Korea Herald* lamented the ongoing complacency, perhaps because of cultural taboos, in addressing the problem.

The creation of 37 memorials to the comfort women in Korea apparently has not stopped this abuse of women, which, as per the *Herald,* has risen over the past decade.[37] Unfortunately, in the United States, domestic violence by Koreans is also a reality. Ironically, one of the enclaves highlighted in a recent *Voice of New York* article on domestic violence in Korean families was Palisades Park, New Jersey, the small northern New Jersey town where the first comfort women monument in America was dedicated in 2010.[38]

---

[33] Jeff Kingston, "'Comfort Women' in South Korea Who Serviced U.S. Forces Seek Justice," *Japan Times*, March 4, 2017, http://www.japantimes.co.jp/opinion/2017/03/04/commentary/comfort-women-south-korea-serviced-u-s-forces-seek-justice/.

[34] Norm Coleman, "President Park Should Publicly Apologize for South Korea's Sexual Violence in Vietnam," *Fox News*, October 13, 2015, http://www.foxnews.com/opinion/2015/10/13/president-park-should-use-us-visit-to-publicly-apologize-for-south-koreas-sexual-violence-in-vietnam.html.

[35] Nicholas Kristof, "Do Korean Husbands Still Beat Their Wives? Definitely," December 5, 1996, http://www.nytimes.com/1996/12/05/world/do-korean-men-still-beat-their-wives-definitely.html.

[36] John Power, "[Voice] Is Domestic Violence Taken Seriously in Korea?, " *The Korea Herald,* May 5, 2012, http://www.koreaherald.com/view.php?ud=20120507001291.

[37] Panda, "Comfort Women Deal Unravels."

[38] Dong Chan Shin, "Domestic Violence in Korean Families," trans. Yehyun Kim,

Japan, the guilty party in the creation of the comfort women system prior to and during WWII, still has its own problems with misogyny as well. In March 2017 the *Japan Times* published an article pointing to the need to stand up to domestic violence inside Japan. It indicated that one of every four Japanese married women reported that they had suffered spousal abuse.[39] These unrepentant trends in both Japan and Korea confirm the persistence of the misogynist views that led to the comfort women system in the first place. There is no evidence that the deploying of comfort women statues has lessened spousal abuse, domestic violence, or the abuse and trafficking of women in South Korea.

Japanese Reactionaries and Korean "Hard-Liners"

Korean hard-liners were angered by the book "Comfort Women of the Empire" (제국의 위안부) published in 2013 by Park Yu-ha, a professor of Japanese literature at Sejong University in Seoul.[40] This anger manifested in the filing of civil and criminal complaints against her.[41] In her book, Park called "for a more comprehensive view of the women in the brothels," and held that "there was no evidence that the Japanese government was officially involved in, and therefore legally responsible for, forcibly recruiting the women from Korea." She stated that Korean collaborators, as well as private Japanese recruiters, "were mainly responsible for placing Korean women, sometimes through coercion, in the 'comfort stations,'" and that some women developed a "comrade like relationship" with Japanese soldiers.[42]

Following publication of her book, Prof. Park was labeled a "pro-Japanese apologist," and found liable for defamation damages in a civil lawsuit in 2016. In January 2017, she prevailed in the criminal case when a judge in the Eastern District Court in Seoul ruled that her academic freedom must be protected.[43]

Voices of NY, December 1, 2014, https://voicesofny.org/2014/12/domestic-violence-korean-families/.

[39] Gilhooly, "Learning to Stand up."

[40] Yu-Ha Park, 제국의 위안부 (Seoul: Dosŏch'ulp'an Ppuri-wa Ip'ari, 2013), https://cldup.com/upJTpO4a_q.pdf.

[41] Choe Sang-Hun, "Professor Who Wrote of Korean 'Comfort Women' Wins Defamation Case," *New York Times*, January 25, 2017, https://www.nytimes.com/2017/01/25/world/asia/korean-comfort-women-park-yu-ha-japan.html?_r=0.

[42] Sang-Hun, "Professor Who Wrote of Korean 'Comfort Women' Wins Defamation Case."

[43] Sang-Hun, "Professor Who Wrote of Korean 'Comfort Women' Wins Defamation Case."

For their part, partisans of the Japanese narrative have also not hesitated to attempt to marginalize those who question their position on the comfort women. For example, they were heartened in 2014 when they could pressure *Asahi Shimbun* to withdraw a series of articles on the comfort women that was based on the false testimony of Seiji Yoshida, who was discredited for fabricating a story involving the transfer of hundreds of Korean women and girls from Korea's Cheju Island to Hainan Island to serve as comfort women. Subsequent to Yoshida's admission of having invented his stories, 2,557 people living in Japan and the United States brought suit in a Tokyo District Court demanding that *Asahi Shimbun* run advertisements in major U.S. newspapers to apologize for the stories. Fifty of the plaintiffs live in the Glendale area. The suit was dismissed, however, on April 27, 2017.[44]

---

[44] Shusuke Murai, "Tokyo Court Rules against Conservative Group Suing Asahi over 'Comfort Women' Articles," *Japan Times*, April 28, 2017, https://www.japantimes.co.jp/news/2016/07/28/national/tokyo-court-rules-conservative-group-suing-asahi-comfort-women-articles/#.WpbgsE2pXVh.

10

The Comfort Women Controversy in the American Public Square

How the Glendale, California Comfort Women Statue Impacts American Lives

The "Statue of Peace" approved by the Glendale, California City Council is a replica of the statue located in front of the Japanese embassy in Seoul. The first line reads, "I was a sex slave of Japanese Military."[1]

During WWII, the U.S. government interned between 110,000 and 120,000 Japanese-Americans under the authority of President Franklin Roosevelt's Executive Order 9066, issued February 19, 1942. Glendale is located 35 minutes by car from Pomona, California where more than 5,000 Japanese-Americans were held in a detention camp between April and September 1942. Some of the young men were later released and joined the U.S. war effort. They number among the most decorated American soldiers in WWII. The 100th Infantry Battalion and the 442nd Regional Combat Team, where such soldiers often served while family members continued to intern in the camps, "earned more than 4,000 Purple Hearts, 560 Silver Stars, seven Presidential Unit Citations and 21 Medals of Honor."[2] The descendants of those herded into the internment camps have been in the United States for at least four generations, unlike the first generation Korean-Americans who

---

[1] Alex More, "Japan Upset about Memorial Honoring WWII Sex Slaves," Death and Taxes, February 27, 2014, https://web.archive.org/web/20171116224003/https://www.deathandtaxesmag.com/215970/japan-upset-about-memorial-honoring-wwii-sex-slaves/.

[2] "American Heroes: Japanese American World War II Nisei Soldiers and the Congressional Gold Medal," Holocaust Museum Houston, https://www.hmh.org/ViewExhibits.aspx?ID=93&ExhibitType=Past.

successfully lobbied for the Glendale statue. There is no evidence that the Glendale Council considered the impact that the quote "I was a sex slave of Japanese Military" might have on the feelings of those Americans of Japanese descent whose parents and grandparents had interned in the camps while their sons risked their lives for their country, the country that had unfairly sequestered and marginalized them. Nowhere in California is there a statue of a young Japanese-American girl that reads, "I was the prisoner of a racist war-time America."

A Narrative in Denial of the U.S. Military's Mistreatment of Japanese Civilians

In 1980 under mounting pressure from the Japanese American Citizens League and other organizations seeking redress, President Jimmy Carter appointed the Commission on Wartime Relocation and Internment of Civilians to investigate the camps. The Commission's report found little evidence of Japanese-American disloyalty at the time of the war. In 1988 Congress passed the Civil Liberties Act of 1988, which apologized for the internment on behalf of the U.S. government and authorized a modest payment to each survivor. However, the apology and reparations did not include the thousands of people of Japanese descent who were abducted from Latin American countries by the U.S. military during WWII. The U.S. government, in fact, targeted over 6,000 men, women, and children of Japanese, German, Italian, and Jewish ancestry in 18 Latin American countries as potentially "dangerous enemy aliens." They were "seized from their homes and communities in those countries by the United States, forcibly deported, stripped of their passports and identity papers, transported over international borders, and imprisoned in concentration camps in the United States."[3] A review of records reveals that there was no specific evidence of subversive activities. Rather, they were to be used in hostage exchanges.[4] Details of their mistreatment were presented to the Inter-American Commission on Human Rights in Washington, D.C. on March 21, 2017. Several lawsuits involving such persons have been dismissed on technical grounds.[5]

The U.S. Military's Untold Use of the Comfort Women System in Japan

In the United States, the inscriptions on the comfort women statues make no

---

[3] *Campaign for Justice: Redress NOW for Japanese Latin Americans* (El Cerrito, CA: National Japanese Historical Society, 2017).

[4] *Preserve and Protect Our Freedoms, 75th Anniversary of Executive Order 9066* (El Cerrito, CA: National Japanese Historical Society, 2017), excerpting *Rafu Shimpo* and *Nichi Bei* newspapers.

[5] *Preserve and Protect Our Freedoms.*

reference to the use of comfort women by the U.S. military in the six months immediately after the war. They also fail to mention the vast complex of camp town brothels set up for American soldiers in Japan and Korea following WWII and the Korean conflict.

Prince Konoe Fumimaro, who served as Japan's Prime Minister during the Pacific War as well as its Deputy Prime Minister at the war's end, insisted that "comfort stations" be made available to arriving troops of the U.S. occupation of Japan following WWII. Japan's provisional leaders during the surrender feared that, with the arrival of the U.S. troops, Japan's young women might be subjected to "mass rape" and thus the need existed to set up a "comfort women system to protect Japanese women and girls."[6] Appealing to Japanese women's sense of patriotism, ads appeared in Japanese newspapers seeking prostitutes to provide sexual services to the arriving U.S. troops:

> We are looking for women of the New Japan who will do their part in rebuilding our nation by doing the important deed of providing comforts for the American forces stationed in Japan. From ages 18 to 25. Shelter, food, and clothing provided.[7]

Because Japanese women were reticent to have contact with foreigners, the government needed to "sweeten the pot" for the women who were to be offered as "gifts from the vanquished."[8] These comfort women received "free of charge – sufficient daily food provisions, such as rice, beef, sugar and cooking oil," which, Yuki Tanaka points out, represented "an extraordinarily attractive offer at a time when the entire population of Japan was suffering from acute food shortages and malnutrition and starvation were widespread."[9] The goal of recruiting these women was to provide a wall of protection for Japan's "respectable women." [10] Besides those recruited directly through these methods, Tanaka points to warnings put in place for recruiters two months after the system's implementation indicating that, just as in the case of the Japanese military comfort women, some of the women who first joined the comfort stations set up for U.S. military "may have been deceived or trapped" into serving as prostitutes.[11] Because of their poverty and the poverty of their families[12], they also found themselves trapped and

---

[6] Tanaka, *Japan's Comfort Women*, 132.
[7] Soh, *The Comfort Women*, 208.
[8] Soh, *The Comfort Women*, 208.
[9] Tanaka, *Japan's Comfort Women*, 136.
[10] Tanaka, *Japan's Comfort Women*, 141.
[11] Tanaka, *Japan's Comfort Women*, 147.
[12] Tanaka, *Japan's Comfort Women*, 155.

"enslaved by loan arrangements"[13] that they accepted for themselves or their families. Tanaka points out that although "little information is available about the cases of high-school students who were deceived or forced to become comfort women," there is, nonetheless, significant circumstantial evidence that Japanese gangster-related organizations played an important role in the post-war effort to "hunt and procure comfort women,"[14] which did reach into the high school girl population that had been working in munitions factories during the war.[15]

Between August 1945 and March 1946, U.S. occupation forces utilized the state-approved brothels the Japanese government had arranged for them. These brothels were assented to by the U.S. military, Tanaka cites a specific case of a U.S. Army General requesting comfort women services for specific dates for his troops and Tanaka maintains that there were other cases of requests by high ranking U.S. military.[16] The comfort stations bore "Shangri-La" style names such as "The International Palace" and "Dream Land." Even some high-ranking U.S. officials who traveled to Japan immediately after the war paid visits to these comfort stations. Under the new American occupation, the name "Special Comfort Facilities Association" was replaced by "Recreation and Amusement Associations (RAAs)."[17]

Anthropologist and comfort women research scholar C. Sarah Soh points to the need to expand accountability beyond Japan for the misogynous acts committed against women in WWII:

> ...the international community, including the United States and other nations of the Allied forces, must acknowledge their complicity in allowing their troops to engage in similar acts and crimes against women in vanquished Japan and postliberation Korea.[18]

By 1945 the war had ended. The day-to-day conditions that put the comfort women located on the war front in life-threatening circumstances no longer existed. Nevertheless, the physical hardship and working conditions that the comfort women faced during the U.S. occupation paralleled those of the WWII comfort stations. Tanaka believes that the major difference was that comfort women mobilized for U.S. troops were properly paid in most cases, whereas

---

[13] Tanaka, *Japan's Comfort Women*, 161.
[14] Tanaka, *Japan's Comfort Women*, 140.
[15] Tanaka, *Japan's Comfort Women*, 138.
[16] Tanaka, *Japan's Comfort Women*, 151.
[17] Tanaka, *Japan's Comfort Women*, 142.
[18] Soh, *The Comfort Women*, 235.

the comfort women mobilized for Japan's military were not.[19] Tanaka points out that at least some of the comfort women used by the U.S. military were Koreans. He references one dinner at a comfort station that allegedly involved U.S. officers and Korean women that carried on until 2 or 3 AM.[20]

More than 10,000 Japanese comfort women were mobilized to service U.S. troops during the period between August 1945 and the end of March 1946. Comfort stations were deployed in all locations in Japan which had large concentrations of U.S. troops, including Tokyo, Osaka, Hiroshima, Okinawa, and Yokohama. In Tokyo alone, "the total number of comfort women and prostitutes gathered to serve the occupation troops at the end of 1945 was 10,000."[21] By October 1945, Hiroshima, at not even one-twentieth the size of Tokyo, had in place some 500 women to staff the comfort stations set up for the U.S. troops and "as expected, 'as soon as they were opened, all comfort stations were crowded with clients.'"[22]

The March 1946 Closure of Comfort Women Stations

On March 25, 1946, the General Headquarters of the Supreme Command designated all brothels, comfort stations, and houses of private prostitution "off-limits" for U.S. military personnel.[23] The unexpected prohibition of patronage by U.S. troops put more than 150,000 Japanese women out of work.[24] The reason for the change in policy was, on the one hand, a concern about the moral degradation of the American military that was outlined in a letter by U.S. military chaplains to General Douglas MacArthur. Furthermore, there was a preponderance of sexually transmitted disease (STDs), including venereal disease (VD) in the comfort women population and in the GIs:

> As many as 200,000 VD cases mainly women in the sex industry were recorded in Japan in 1946. The majority of these women's clients were occupation troops. The brothels that the troops patronized were sanctioned both by the Japanese and Allied occupation authorities...[25]

Tanaka writes that "in March, 1946, the average VD rate for the entire U.S. occupation troops was 274 per 1,000; in other words, more than one in every

---

[19] Tanaka, *Japan's Comfort Women*, 147.
[20] Tanaka, *Japan's Comfort Women*, 86–87.
[21] Tanaka, *Japan's Comfort Women*, 154.
[22] Tanaka, *Japan's Comfort Women*, 136–137.
[23] Tanaka, *Japan's Comfort Women*, 162.
[24] Tanaka, *Japan's Comfort Women*, 162.
[25] Tanaka, *Japan's Comfort Women*, 160.

four GIs was suffering from some form of VD."[26]

The U.S. Failure to Provide Justice for Comfort Women

The vast majority of the WWII comfort women were of Asian rather than European heritage, which has led to allegations that, unlike the case involving European women as comfort women where the tried and convicted Japanese military officer responsible was executed, the cases against Japan for use of Asian women were dismissed, presumably because Asian women were viewed as less important.[27] A prevalent mindset existed among both the Japanese and American military alike that women were expected to provide sexual services to the soldiers:

> A common refrain is the idea that women are morally obliged to offer amenities to soldiers who are fighting at the risk of their lives, to defend their people and the nation. This kind of androcentric ideology has been, and still is, deeply rooted in most military forces and the societies that support them.[28]

This misogynist mindset also found itself reflected in the ways in which American soldiers treated the Japanese women doing clerical or translation work for the occupation forces. Tanaka cites numerous examples but this example confirms one's worst speculation:

> In the case of one military site, the troops had assembled photos of the Japanese women working there. Those with a cross above the photo were women who had been "seduced" by one or more members of the U.S. military. Out of 200 photos posted there, according to one of the interpreters, only ten did not have the cross mark and these were "all newly employed women." [29]

Tanaka cites scores of examples of Japanese women workers who were sexually assaulted by GIs.[30]

---

[26] Tanaka, *Japan's Comfort Women*, 161–162.
[27] Tanaka, *Japan's Comfort Women*, 87.
[28] Tanaka, *Japan's Comfort Women*, 87.
[29] Tanaka, *Japan's Comfort Women*, 130.
[30] Tanaka, *Japan's Comfort Women*, 111–166.

The American Leadership's Attitudes on Sex and the U.S. Soldier

In 1945 a Catholic priest contacted New York Senator Robert Wagner and New York Congressman Hamilton Fish to report an attitude prevalent among U.S. military that "it's necessary for a man to satisfy his desires, especially a married man."[31] As with the Japanese military in WWII, a popular view existed in the American military that, through controlled prostitution, it would be possible to reduce the spread of venereal disease. The American brass also felt that prostitution served as a "means to improve troop morale with relative safety." [32] Tanaka cites many cases of alleged rapes of Japanese women by members of the U.S. military. In Yokohama, a large city southeast of Tokyo, the city police reported 119 cases of rape of Japanese women by U.S. military between September and October 1945. Tanaka speculates that this represents less rather than the real number of cases; Japanese had reservations about reporting cases of rape of Japanese women to the U.S. military. They feared that it would cause more trouble for informants rather than improve the conditions that Japanese women faced.

Sharp censorship of any report of alleged malfeasance by United States troops was observed, based on guidelines released by the U.S. military leadership on September 19, 1945, which read that "there shall be no destructive criticism of the Allied Forces Occupation and nothing which might invite mistrust or resentment of the troops." [33] Comfort women researcher C. Sarah Soh observes that "the atrocities of Japan's imperial army against women have been amply aired in recent years, but few people in the United States are aware of heinous sexual crimes committed by American military men, most of which went unpublished due to the unequal Status of Forces Agreement (SOFA) between the superpower United States and Korea." [34]

Voluntary or Forced Conscription into Sexual Service for the U.S. Military

One of many cases cited by Tanaka illustrates this tragic reality. This case involved a dozen young women conscripted into the system who had lost their parents and families in the Hiroshima bombing. Tanaka describes the incident:

---

[31] Tanaka, *Japan's Comfort Women*, 106.
[32] Tanaka, *Japan's Comfort Women*, 109.
[33] Tanaka, *Japan's Comfort Women*, 124–125.
[34] Soh, *The Comfort Women*, 214.

A dozen high-school students, who were members of the Women's Volunteer Corps, were staying in a dormitory of one of the arsenals in Kure, a major naval port in Hiroshima prefecture. They had become war orphans when, on August 6, 1945, their families had perished and their homes had been destroyed by the atomic bomb. (Shortly after the bombing of Hiroshima, the younger sister of one of the dormitory students, Momoyama Chikako, had made the trip from Hiroshima to Kure on foot, only to fall dead in front of the factory gate on arrival due to radiation exposure.) As the students had nowhere to return to, they stayed at the dormitory, doing domestic work for the factory manager's family. One day, the above mentioned Yoneyama appeared at the factory, and gave the factory manager several tons of sugar and some packets of foreign-made cigarettes. Then the factory manager took Yoneyama to the dormitory. Yoneyama told the students about a 'task' – the same 'task' about which he had told the students in Kawasaki. They were put into a truck and taken away. First they were taken into a house in an unknown place where they were gang-raped by a number of GIs, and then were taken by the same truck to a building in another place they were again gang-raped by a different group of GIs. Eventually they were taken to a comfort station and attended to by a medic of the occupation troops. A few days later all were found to be infected with VD. [35]

A survey of prostitutes conducted by Tokyo Police Headquarters in 1948 revealed that 13% of those interviewed had lost both their parents during WWII or in the period immediately following the war.[36]

---

[35] Tanaka, *Japan's Comfort Women*, 139–140.
[36] Tanaka, *Japan's Comfort Women*, 155.

11

The Implications of Establishing a Comfort Women Memorial in the United States or Europe

Complicity in Defending the Guilty and Discounting the Innocent

The United States chose not to prosecute the officials responsible for the comfort women system. For the United States occupation forces in Japan after WWII, the priority for prosecution and punishment were Class A War Criminals, guilty of so-called "Crimes against the Peace," referring to those Japanese leaders who had planned and attacked the United States and its allies at the start of the war. The United States under the leadership of Supreme Commander Douglas MacArthur made the decision **not** to investigate or prosecute the perpetrators of the comfort women system, despite having testimonies and physical evidence available to them that established beyond a reasonable doubt that the system had existed and was operated by the Japanese military with the support of other branches of government, including the Ministry of Foreign Affairs.

The end of WWII marked the start of the Cold War. Soviet protégés quickly seized power across Central and Eastern Europe. In East Asia, Kim Il Sung, with Soviet support, soon rose to power in North Korea, based on a hasty agreement between the United States and the USSR that ceded Korea north of the 38th parallel to Soviet influence in return for Soviet entry into WWII three months after the end of the war on the European front, just one week prior to Japan's surrender. In 1949 Mao Tse Tung and his supporters also emerged as the victors in China.

In the case of the European front, both the United States and the Soviet Union arranged clemency and safe passage for some key German actors in the war, especially scientists and spies. These individuals received their freedom or reduced sentences in exchange for valuable information related to Germany's advanced missile and nuclear weaponry development and other strategic intelligence. In the case of Japan, the United States, witnessing the new threat posed by the Soviet Union and its rising Asian allies, offered clemency in exchange for information to Japanese researchers who were responsible for horrible atrocities against Chinese civilians in the infamous Unit 731 where Japan tested biological and chemical weapons on Chinese citizens.

The United States also rehabilitated some Japanese political leaders soon after the war including Prime Minister Nobusuke Kishi, who had served as Minister of Commerce and Industry in the Cabinet of War of Prime Minister Hideki Tojo, who had ordered the attack on Pearl Harbor in 1941. Kishi was arrested at the end of the war and spent three years in prison where he awaited trial as an alleged Class A War Criminal. The United States identified him as someone who could play a productive role in the future of Japan and in defending the Pacific from the threat of the Soviet Union and its emerging Asian allies.[1] He was released and would eventually become Prime Minister. Prime Minister Kishi was but one among numerous individuals who had served in the Tojo cabinet and the Japanese military yet eventually joined the U.S.-Japan partnership. What do officials in the United States need to be aware of as they contemplate whether or not to establish a memorial for the comfort women?

Municipal, state, and federal officials in today's America have given their approval to the monuments in their jurisdictions. These memorials recall the tribulation endured by thousands of victims of the Japanese military's comfort women system during and prior to WWII. The memorials single out Japan for creating and implementing the system that trafficked these women and girls against their will and forever tarnished their integrity and quality of life.

Charges against Japan for its role in creating and presiding over the dehumanizing conditions of the comfort women system are justified. Nevertheless, the anti-Japan rather than the pro-comfort women narrative advanced by CSOs in the United States, such as the KAFC and the Chinese-American Comfort Women Justice Coalition, do not further reconciliation and healing. For its part, the narrative advanced by the Global Alliance for

---

[1] Clyde Haberman, "Nobusuke Kishi, Ex-Tokyo Leader," *New York Times*, August 8, 1987, http://www.nytimes.com/1987/08/08/obituaries/nobusuke-kishi-ex-tokyo-leader.html.

Historical Truth (GAHT), which supports Japanese ultranationalist views on the comfort women conveniently rejects the manifest evidence of Japan's central role in creating the comfort women system.

This bitter battle of narratives jeopardizes efforts by the United States and the democracies of Japan and Korea to promote rule of law and democratic values in East Asia at a time when China remains ambivalent about the value of the rule of law versus the dictates of the Communist Party.

Americans who hold office in the local, state, or federal government need not choose between the politicized, carefully crafted narratives of the supporters and detractors of the comfort women statues. Indeed, American local government officials asked to choose between these two narratives should be aware that the United States, not Japan, decided against prosecuting those responsible for the creation and implementation of the comfort women system. Those Japanese responsible for the coercive recruitment and assignment of Dutch women to comfort stations were tried after the war and the leader in this, Japanese Army Major Keiji Okada, was executed for his role.[2] It was an American choice not to show the same judicial vigilance towards those responsible for crimes against Asian women.

The United States has been an active actor in the comfort women issue. U.S. military leadership allowed American military forces to use the comfort women system between August 1945 and March 1946. The U.S. Supreme Command censored the press in Japan and Korea for decades after the war, prohibiting newspapers from reporting on the thousands of cases of sexual assault and rape allegedly committed by U.S. military forces during the occupation of Japan. For 72 years, ten times longer than the existence of Japan's comfort station system, the U.S. military has enabled and patronized a massive prostitution ring in East Asia, which has compromised the integrity of young women from Japan, Korea, and the Philippines. Many of these women have also been deceived and trafficked against their will under circumstances similar to those faced by the comfort women during World War. Commenting on this, Dr. Yuki Tanaka, one of the pioneers in exposing Japan's comfort women system, has undertaken a critical study of both Japan's WWII comfort women system and what followed under the American occupation. Tanaka critically assesses the status and social conditions of Asia's women since the U.S. occupation and argues that "far from implementing 'democratization policies,'" for women, the U.S. occupation "actively participated in their subjugation."[3]

---

[2] "Women Made to Become Comfort Women—Netherlands," Asian Women's Fund, http://www.awf.or.jp/e1/netherlands.html.

[3] Tanaka, *Japan's Comfort Women*, 165.

Should monuments in the United States ignore the camp town brothels that have surrounded U.S. military camps in Korea for more than 70 years? Should memorials in the United States conceal that many of the women suffering this abuse today are young Filipina women, typically deceived by Korean and Japanese *entremetteurs* into coming to Korea and Japan?[4] Like the original Korean and Taiwanese comfort women, young Filipinas are being promised positions as servers and entertainers, only to find themselves forced to serve as indentured sex workers.[5] If the United States' role in this terrible chapter of history was revealed, the monuments would do far more good than they do presently by engaging solely in Japan bashing.

In the case of the comfort women, the United States was not only neglectful in failing to undertake sufficient investigation and to seek justice for the victims but it also patronized the system in the first six months of the U.S. occupation of Japan. The United States numbers among the culpable actors in this tragic chapter of history not only because of its use of the comfort women system after the war but because of U.S. forces' continued patronage of a vast prostitution network across Korea and Japan since then. Omitting reference to American participation in the comfort women tragedy is akin to an American city erecting a monument that denounces the treatment of African slaves by the Dutch or Portuguese during their transport to the United States while ignoring the horrors that they faced once they arrived here.

---

[4] "Court Rules in Favor," *Korea JoongAng Daily*.
[5] "Court Rules in Favor," *Korea JoongAng Daily*.

Closing Thoughts

Since beginning our research on this topic in 2014, our work on this book has taken us to Japan, Korea, Taiwan, and across the United States. It has led us to conclude that in most cases the comfort women were deceptively recruited, and in some cases they were abducted. They were sexually violated and suffered unimaginable physical and psychological abuse. Sadly, the chapters that followed in their lives were largely defined by these experiences.

Our research has led us to conclude that the main actors responsible for this are the Japanese militarists who implemented and subsequently concealed the system, exploiting the women they coerced to staff it. Yet responsibility does not lie with the Japanese alone. It also lies with the Koreans, Taiwanese, and Chinese who benefited by recruiting for or managing the comfort women system. It also lies with those who, like the non-German supporters of Nazism, supported the Asian Co-Prosperity Sphere that required militarization and other "sacrifices" to defeat Western colonialism and replace it with Japan's own empire. Fault also lies with the American occupation leaders who downplayed and dismissed evidence of the system, assented to the United States military's 1945-46 use of comfort women, and permit the still ongoing use of camp town brothels where young Asian women have served as prostitutes for GIs and sex tourists for the past eight decades.

The U.S. monuments memorializing the suffering of the WWII comfort women do not address the broader penumbra of culpability related to the comfort women system. They only indicate Japan's culpability. They do not address the misogynist mindset that enabled the system. They make no mention of the major role played by Korean and Taiwanese collaborators who deceptively recruited the young female victims, promising them education and professional development rather than the fate that actually awaited these women. The statues also make no mention of America's role in perpetuating the comfort women system following WWII. The cities establishing the memorials fail to take into account how the alliance among Japan, Korea, and the United States is affected by creating anti-Japan memorials that attribute culpability to a single source, while in reality numerous Koreans, Chinese, and Americans also hold responsibility for the abuse of Asian women during and following the war.

The sexual and psychological abuse that women suffered due to the comfort women system constituted an egregious violation of human rights. However, American monuments recollecting this tragic chapter of history need to tell a more complete and honest story than what we find in places such as Fairfax, Virginia, Palisades Park, New Jersey, and Glendale, California, which only focus on Japan. Just as Germany had its non-German "Ivans" who tortured and killed the victims in the death camps, Japan's militarists had their share of supporters who were neither Japanese in nationality nor in ethnicity but who deceived, coerced, and abused the victims of the comfort women system. Koreans should not downplay the major role that Korean agents played in recruiting the victims and in helping to manage them, and Americans should recognize their role in the prolongation and patronization of the comfort women system and the cover-up that prevented prosecution of the guilty parties. The decision not to prosecute those responsible for the comfort women system was made by U.S.-led occupation forces at the end of WWII, and the U.S. military's patronage of the vast, exploitative network of prostitution in Japan, Korea, and the Philippines which began after WWII continues to this day. China is also implicated. Thousands of young Korean women are deceptively promised refuge from the suffering of North Korea and travel to China only to be forced into a modern comfort women system where they are sold as brides or find themselves forced to work in brothels for years to pay the debt incurred to China-based trafficking rings. These women serve as indentured sex workers and face miserable lives and endless humiliation. The broader context of events that we mention here needs to be taken into consideration when the comfort women question is examined outside of Japan and Korea.

We believe that the acceptance and acknowledgement of the materials presented in this book will encourage introspection; it will hopefully inspire thoughtful initiatives to address the longstanding cultural assumptions and institutions in Asia and America alike that have demeaned women and contributed to their victimization in the past as well as in the present. The time has come to address these attitudes, rather than allow this historical tragedy to be used by reckless nationalists and self-serving politicians be they Japanese, Korean, Chinese or American.

Note on Indexing

E-IR's publications do not feature indexes. If you are reading this book in paperback and want to find a particular word or phrase you can do so by downloading a free PDF version of this book from the E-International Relations website.

View the e-book in any standard PDF reader such as Adobe Acrobat Reader (pc) or Preview (mac) and enter your search terms in the search box. You can then navigate through the search results and find what you are looking for. In practice, this method can prove much more targeted and effective than consulting an index.

If you are using apps (or devices) to read our e-books, you should also find word search functionality in those.

You can find all of our e-books at: http://www.e-ir.info/publications

www.ingramcontent.com/pod-product-compliance
Lightning Source LLC
Chambersburg PA
CBHW070118110526
44587CB00015BA/2211